Essay Index

STORIES OF
GREAT CRAFTSMEN

THE STONING OF ST STEPHEN
Carved in wood by Grinling Gibbons
Victoria and Albert Museum

STORIES OF
GREAT CRAFTSMEN

BY
S. H. GLENISTER

WITH ILLUSTRATIONS IN HALF-TONE AND LINE

Essay Index

Essay Index Reprint Series

BOOKS FOR LIBRARIES PRESS
FREEPORT, NEW YORK

First Published 1939
Reprinted 1970

THIS BOOK
IS
DEDICATED TO
JOHN, AGED SIX, AND DAVID, AGED TWO,
WITH THE HOPE THAT, IN LATER YEARS,
IT WILL HELP THEM TO APPRECIATE
THE WORK OF GREAT CRAFTSMEN AT ITS
TRUE VALUE

INTERNATIONAL STANDARD BOOK NUMBER:
0-8369-1831-2

LIBRARY OF CONGRESS CATALOG CARD NUMBER:
75-128247

PRINTED IN THE UNITED STATES OF AMERICA

NOTE

IN order to make the stories interesting to readers, imagination has been resorted to in providing some of the dialogue and connecting links between important events in each life; especially is this so in the story of the boyhood of Thomas Chippendale, about which the available information is very meagre. However, great care has been taken to represent the important facts of each story accurately.

The author desires to acknowledge his indebtedness to the many writers whose books he has made use of to obtain material facts for these stories.

Thanks are due to Mr J. F. Middleton, B.Sc., for kindly reading the proofs.

S.H.G.

CONTENTS

ILLUSTRATIONS

11

STORIES OF GREAT CRAFTSMEN

I

GUTENBERG AND CAXTON
Pioneers of Printing

CAN you imagine what it would be like to live in a world which contained no books, papers, periodicals, or anything which you could read? It would be terribly dull, don't you think? It is difficult to realize what we would do in our spare time without something to read. But this was how people lived until about 500 years ago. Of course, books would have been useless to them, because very few were able to read and write; and those few were mainly the monks who lived and worked in the monasteries.

A SCRIBE COPYIST

You might wonder, then, how people got to know the news of events taking place in other parts of the world if there were no papers or wireless sets to inform them. This was conveyed through the towns and villages in a curious way by men called minstrels. These minstrels were really tramping singers who wandered far and wide, picking up any scraps of news that came their way. Whenever a minstrel was seen to arrive at a village, the villagers would gather

13

outside the local hostelry and would listen while the minstrel sang his songs to them. The words of these songs told the news of things that had happened since the minstrel was last in the village. The money he collected from his audiences provided him with food and lodging.

The rich barons sometimes received their news more quickly by letters from their friends, but most of them were too ignorant to read and employed monks and clerks to tell them what the letters contained and to write replies. The monks also used to write tales and stories to amuse these barons, but these had to be written in ink on parchment, which was a very laborious task. Consequently only one or two copies of each story would be written, which made them very expensive and rare.

This state of ignorance might possibly have lasted until the present day if a person by the name of John Gutenberg had not been born in Mainz, in Germany, in the year 1398. For he was the first man in Europe to discover the art of printing from movable types, whereby many copies of a single piece of writing could be produced at reasonable cost.

John's parents were rich people at the time of his birth, but a few years later, the poor people of Mainz had a quarrel with the rich ones and took away their wealth. In despair the well-to-do folk fled from Mainz, and many, including the Gutenbergs, settled in another town called Strassburg.

John grew up to be a clever boy who was very interested in experimenting with new ideas. We first hear of him as the inventor of a new kind of looking-glass which was so much admired by his friends that they urged him to start a business for making and selling them to the great ladies of the land. He mentioned it to his parents, but they could not give him enough money to buy tools and materials for his needs. Eventually he met a man named

Dritzhen who was so interested in the idea that he lent John the necessary money and became his partner in business. This business prospered for about twelve years until a stroke of bad luck ruined it. John had heard of a great pilgrimage that was shortly to assemble at a near-by town called Aix-la-Chapelle, and he said to his partner:

"As there will be thousands of people coming from far and wide to attend this pilgrimage, we shall be able to earn much money by selling them our mirrors."

His partner agreed, and they set to work and made thousands of these mirrors, using all the money they had to buy the materials. Then they received a stunning blow. The pilgrimage was postponed. No people came to buy their mirrors, and the business had to be given up through lack of money.

So, without money, John had to look for other work to do. He had for some time been interested in trying to print numerous copies of a drawing or picture without the necessity of drawing each one separately. His first idea was to carve a picture on the surface of a block of wood, smear the carved part with ink, and then press it on to a piece of paper. When the block was removed, he found that an impression of the drawing had been transferred to the paper. You can see how useful this was. To obtain, say, one hundred copies of the picture, all he had to do was to ink the block each time previous to pressing it against a sheet of paper. Gutenberg was so satisfied with this invention of his that he thought writing could be multiplied in the same way. So he began experiments with words.

He first obtained a block of wood as large as a page, and on it he carved rows and rows of words, each word in its correct place, so that the printed page would be readable. This idea again worked very well, but it was expensive to make a book this way, because it took so long to carve out each separate page. Eventually, after much thought, he decided that it would be better to make a separate block for each letter in the alphabet, and then

he could combine the letters into any words he desired. He started on fresh experiments. First he carved on hundreds of blocks of wood numerous copies of each letter—more of some than others. For instance, he would need more A's than Z's, so he cut fifty copies of the letter A to every one of the letter Z. He then made a frame, the size of a page of a book, in which to hold the letters. As he fitted the words into the frame he placed a thinner plain block of wood between each word to space them out, and similarly he placed strips of wood between the rows of words to separate them. When all the words were fixed tightly in the frame, all he had to do to obtain numerous copies of the page was to ink the surface of the frame each time he pressed it on a piece of paper.

This method worked well, but Gutenberg still found it difficult to start printing properly because he had no money. He went to a merchant by the name of Fust and asked him to lend him the money. Fust was a very shrewd business-man who was always ready to lend money to anyone if he thought he could obtain good profits for

16

himself from the bargain. Gutenberg interested him
greatly in his new idea of printing, so he agreed to lend
him 800 guilders, providing that if anything went wrong
with the business he was to have all the tools and printing-
equipment that Gutenberg was to buy and make with
the aid of the money.

So the business was started. Gutenberg could not do it
all himself, so he engaged a metal-worker named Peter
Schoeffer to help him. They started printing pages of
words, which they sold to the rich people in the district.
It was found, after the wooden blocks had been in use for
some time, that they soon wore out with continual inking
and pressing. This is where Schoeffer came in useful to
Gutenberg. He noticed how the blocks were beginning
to wear so that the letters were smudged and uneven
when printed on the paper, so he said to Gutenberg,
"These blocks will not last us long. We need something
harder than wood to make them from. Let us try to cut
some in a soft metal."

They found it very difficult to cut numerous letters on
small blocks of metal, so another idea struck them. They
carved a letter A on the end of a block of metal and used
it to punch a hollow impression of the letter in another
piece of metal. Then all they had to do was to melt some
of a softer metal in a ladle and pour it into the hollow.
When it had set hard it was taken out and was found
to be a perfect copy of the original letter A. They could
then make as many copies of the letter as they wished by
pouring more molten metal into the mould as soon as the
previous lot had set hard enough to be taken out. This
method is really the one that is still used to-day, although,
of course, the ways of doing it have been greatly improved.

When Gutenberg and Schoeffer had finished making
enough letters to start printing properly, the former found
that he had not enough money left to pay wages and

obtain more materials. So, in the hour of his triumph, it looked as though he must close the business. But Fust came to his aid again and lent him another 800 guilders. Fust did not do this out of generosity, but he saw that the idea was so good that eventually he must reap in large profits from it himself. However, Gutenberg decided to set himself the colossal task of printing the complete Bible in Latin.

A PAGE FROM A BOOK PRINTED BY
GUTENBERG AND FUST ABOUT 1450

After much work and difficulty the Bible was finished in the year 1455, bound up into two great volumes. By this time the few dukes and lords who had taken the trouble to learn to read were keen to see the first book made by this new process, and Gutenberg's bibles sold very quickly. Everybody was amazed at their cheapness and clearness of type, and all agreed that the pages of print 'were as clear as handwriting and easier to read.'

Gutenberg was very happy at the reception his book had received from the learned people, but his joy was soon marred by the greedy moneylender, Fust. This man now asked for all the money back which he had lent to Gutenberg. He knew that Gutenberg could not pay it, but he wanted to steal his invention now that it was on the way to earning a lot of money. Gutenberg tried all means to keep Fust from taking his precious printing-materials from him, but it was of no use. Fust seized the lot. Of course, he had a right to do this, because that was part of the bargain when he lent Gutenberg the money; but it was very mean of him to take advantage of it in Gutenberg's hour of triumph.

After this great blow, Gutenberg did not do much more, although it is thought by some that he set up another printing-press later and printed one or two more books. He died in the year 1468 without money or friends, but he has achieved lasting fame as the first man to print a book.

While Gutenberg was spending his last days in poverty, Fust and Schoeffer were becoming famous throughout Europe, and nobles from various countries were buying their books.

At about this time there was living in England a lad named William Caxton. He was born in Tenterden, in Kent, in 1411. His parents were well-to-do and were connected with many of the great families of England of that time—so much so that they sent him to school to learn to read and write, a very unusual thing for parents to do in those days. We know that he went to school, because in a letter he once wrote he put, "I lerned myn englissh in kente in the weeld," and at another time he wrote thanking his mother and father for "setteing hym to schole."

At the age of sixteen he was sent to London to work for a rich silk mercer, from whom he was to learn his trade of dealing in silks. The mercers, at that time, were a famous body of business men, and Robert Large, to whom William was sent, was one of the most important. William was made an apprentice to Mr Large. That means that he had to agree to work faithfully for his master and do his best to learn the business in which he was engaged, for a period of seven years. In return his master had to promise to feed him, clothe him, and teach him well and truly his art and craft.

So William lived in his master's house as one of the family. His master was very kind to him and treated him as though he were a son. Many famous people, such as nobles and kings, were interested in trading and often came to stay at Mr Large's house to discuss business. Sometimes William was allowed the privilege of sitting and talking with them. In this way he learned much about foreign countries and other peoples which otherwise he could never have known.

He also became very interested in reading and often used to spend his spare time in his master's library of manuscripts, browsing through the sheets of parchment and translating the Latin and French writings into his own language. He became a great scholar and often spent time translating manuscripts for his master's friends.

Towards the end of William's apprenticeship his master died. He had admired the boy so much, however, that William found himself the possessor of £150, a legacy left to him in the will.

As his apprenticeship was not over when Mr Large died, William had to be found other work under the terms of the agreement. Consequently he was sent to Bruges, in Belgium. Bruges, at that time, was the centre of the woollen- and silk-trade. All the great merchants from every country used to gather there to do their buying and selling.

He soon started a business of his own, and it prospered greatly. By the time he was twenty-eight years old he was fairly wealthy. He was greatly liked and respected by the other merchants residing in Bruges, and eventually he became the leader of all the traders, being given the title of 'Governor of the English Nation beyond the Seas.' In this office he became friends with many famous people, such as the Duke of Burgundy. So friendly was he with this Duke that he was allowed the free use of his library, which was reputed to be the finest in the world. He told the Duke that he found "grete pleasyr and delyte in reading strange and mervayllous historyes."

The Duke was also a great lover of literature, and he employed many writers and translators to enrich the shelves of his great library. Seeing that Caxton was so keenly interested in this kind of work, the Duke's wife, the Duchess Margaret, took him into her employ to help with the writing. In this way he got to know the other clever writers working for the Duke.

One day one of these writers said to Caxton, "Have you heard the news spreading abroad from the land of Germany that a citizen of Mainz, by name of Gutenberg, has performed a new mode of writing without the hand. It is greatly marvellous if accounts be truly given. The writing is executed on pieces of metal, which, when collected together in orderly fashion and then coated with inks, will produce a limitless number of like manuscripts without the labour of handwriting. Books made by like methods do, I am told, cost but little money to buy."

Caxton was keenly interested in this new invention and mentioned it to his employer, the Duchess of Burgundy. She sent him to Germany to see if the stories about this new kind of printing were true. He travelled to Cologne and there found one of the new printing-presses in operation, so he decided to become an apprentice again and learn this marvellous new craft. With the help of the 'lady Margarete' he was given permission by the burgomaster of Cologne to stay in the town long enough to acquire this new learning. He afterwards wrote that he spent his time there "practysing and lerning at my grete charge and dispense" all the work involved in printing.

When he had gathered together all the knowledge he could, he returned to Bruges and built a printing-press there in partnership with a man named Colard Mansion. There Caxton printed a number of books, some of which he had either written or translated himself.

But by the time his press was well established, he was feeling an urge to return to England. He had been in foreign parts for nearly thirty years now, and he was yearning to return and settle down. The desire had also come to him to give to the English people books which were written in their native language. This, he thought, would make it easier for them to learn to read and write. Finally, after much hesitation he sold his partnership in the printing-press at Bruges and set sail for England. On landing he journeyed to London to find a suitable house in which he could start his printing again. It seems that he was not satisfied with the unoccupied premises there, because he took a house in Westminster which was, at that time, a town distinct from London City.

The house belonged to Westminster Abbey and had a sign called the 'Red Pale' over the door. That is why Caxton's first printing-press is often spoken of as being "at the sign of the Red Pale in Westminster."

He soon made a stock of metal letters and set up a wooden press in which to print the pages. With the help of a young assistant, named Wynkyn de Worde, whom he had brought with him from Bruges, he began to print small pamphlets. As these pamphlets began to be distributed, the nobles showed great enthusiasm for this new vogue of mechanical writing called printing. The highest in the land were clamouring to buy his books. Caxton's press became very busy. The first book he ever printed at Westminster was a translation of a French book called *The Sayings of the Philosophers*, and it was dated November 18, 1477. Another early book taught one how to play the game of chess, a popular pastime among the rich, and it was called *The Game and Playe of the Chesse*.

Caxton's books began to sell so quickly to the upper classes that he had to employ two more assistants, Richard Pynson and Robert Copland.

Caxton then began to illustrate the pages of his books with pictures. These were done by Gutenberg's method of wood blocks on which the pictures were engraved. This method is still often used by some of our great artists to-day for reproducing their work. They use chisels and gouges to cut out the pictures on the highly polished ends of blocks of boxwood. Beautiful prints can then be obtained by using these blocks in a printing-press.

The actual print in the first few books that were produced at Westminster was not very good, considering modern standards, and the assistants soon began to improve the metal type. Wynkyn de Worde made a new fount—that means a complete set of metal letters—which gave much greater clearness to the printed words. Then Richard Pynson, one of the newer assistants, made a fount of the kind of type we now use for our books and newspapers, called roman type. And so the business progressed.

By this time Caxton was leaving most of the printing-work to his assistants, while he gave more time to writing tales of chivalry and short stories and translating well-known foreign manuscripts.

In 1477 the Caxton Press produced a book called *Jason*, which, with the permission of the King and Queen, he presented to the Young Prince of Wales so that "he may begynne to lerne to rede Englisshe."

A considerable number of books were printed before the year 1480, and one book, called *The Horse, The Sheep, and The Goose*, was sold so quickly that it had to be reprinted.

It is rather interesting to know that Caxton printed the first advertisement to be known in England. He posted small bills in different places to tell people about a book he had just finished. The bills read something like this:

"If it plese ony man to bye one of this present book, whiche ben wel and truly correct, late hym come to westmonester in to the almonsrye at the reed pale and he shall have them good chepe."

I wonder if you are able to read all the words? The old spelling looks very strange to us. But Caxton seemed to spell his words in different ways in each book. For instance, in one book he mentions some work which he did for the Abbot of Westminster. The Abbot, having a high regard for Caxton's work, asked him to copy and print in the new roman type the story that had been written on a precious manuscript, and this is what Caxton wrote about it:

"My lord abbot of westmynster ded do show to me certayn evydenses wryton in olde englysshe for to reduce it in to our englysshe now usid."

Have you noticed the different spellings of the word Westminster in the two pieces of Caxton's writing?

Caxton went on working right up to the day of his death in 1491. He had often written pamphlets on the subject of idleness, but it would be impossible to accuse Caxton of being idle himself, for in the fourteen years he worked at "The Sign of the Red Pale" he published more than ninety books and printed about 18,000 pages. This

no drede ne fere no thynge/ For I shalle not accuse the / For I
shalle shelve to hym another way/ And as the hunter came/
he demaunded of the sheepherd yf he had sene the wulf pas-
se / And the sheepherd both with the hede and of the eyen she-
wed to the hunter the place where the wulf was / & with the
hand and the tongue shelved alle the contrarye / And in
contynent the hunter vnderstood hym wel / But the wulf
whiche percyued wel all the fayned maners of the sheepherd
fled awey/ ¶ And within a lytyll whyle after the sheepherd
encountred and mette with the wulf/ to whome he sayd/ paye
me of that I haue kepte the secrete/ ¶ And thenne the wulf
answerd to hym in this manere / I thanke thyn handes and
thy tongue/ and not thyn hede ne thyn eyen / For by them I
shold haue ben bytrayd/ yf I had not fledde awey/ ¶ And
therfore men must not truste in hym that hath two faces and
two tongues/ for suche folke is lyke and semblable to the scor-
pion/ the whiche enoynteth with his tongue/ and prycketh sore with his taylle

A Page from Æsop's Fables printed by Caxton in 1483
British Museum

was an astonishing achievement when one considers the primitive nature of the equipment with which he worked. But it is not so much the amount or the quality of the work which makes us honour the name of the great craftsman: more is-it for the reason that he brought to England the invention of printing—one of the greatest blessings of civilization.

At Caxton's death, his chief assistant, Wynkyn de Worde, became master of the Westminster press and carried on the good work of giving to the English people books by which they might learn to read and enjoy their leisure hours. During his ownership of the business he printed more than 400 books. By this time printing was making great advances, and other men had learned the art. One man named Thomas Rood had started a press in Oxford, another press was set up in St Albans, and others had been opened in Scotland. Printing had come to stay. The writers of manuscripts were needed no longer, and many turned their talents to the art of printing.

As time went on, more of the common people began to learn to read these printed pamphlets, and the Government became alarmed. They were afraid that the people would begin to learn about the careless ways in which they were being governed; they were afraid that the people might rise in rebellion if they learned too much or read pamphlets telling them the news of the horrible persecutions being carried out on innocent men. So in 1530 a law was passed making it a crime to print anything with which the Government did not agree. This ban on the printer's freedom caused the craft to decline for a time, but its progress could not be held down for good. New inventions were continually being added to the simple presses; type and paper were improved so that the art of printing has become one of the marvels of the modern age. The workshops of our newspapers now have printing-presses, enormous in size and intricate in construction, which are capable of printing more than 120,000 eighteen-page newspapers every hour they are running! And only one man is needed to set up and watch each great press as it works, smoothly and speedily printing and folding in correct order, page after page of our morning newspaper, at a pace faster than the eye can see. This might never have been possible but for the great minds and craftsmanship of Gutenberg and Caxton.

II

SIR CHRISTOPHER WREN
Architect

DURING the reign of King Charles I a clergyman named Dr Christopher Wren was the rector of the church in the

SIR CHRISTOPHER WREN
National Portrait Gallery

village of East Knoyle, Wiltshire. He was the father of two children; the first, Christopher, who is the hero of this story, was born in the year 1632, and his sister, Susan, five years earlier.

Dr Wren was a very learned and accomplished man.

28

Besides his ordinary work he was interested in scientific study and was one of the earliest members of that now famed body of distinguished scientists, the Royal Society. He also knew much about the art of building and architecture, and it is said that with his own hands he decorated the walls of his church at East Knoyle with borders of beautiful plaster carvings of flowers, figures, and scripture texts.

Christopher, his son, also showed great ability at a very early age. He was rather a delicate child and spent most of his time indoors learning how to read and write. By the time he was seven he could read and write well in both English and Latin. This was a truly remarkable accomplishment for such a young child, especially in those days when there was such little opportunity for education of any kind. Christopher was fortunate to have such a learned father to teach him. He was also lucky to be able to learn to do arithmetic and geometry in his early years. This was possible because his sister Susan married another clergyman, named the Rev. William Holder, who was an expert at mathematics. He used to spend an hour each day helping Christopher with his lessons.

When Christopher was nine he composed a poem in Latin and gave it to his father on New Year's Day. It is a very clever piece of work for one so young. Its English translation reads:

> To you, Deare Sir, your Son presenteth heare,
> The firstfruits of his pains and of the Yeare;
> Which may (though small) in time a harvest grow
> If you to cherish these your favour shew.

A year later his father decided that it was time Christopher went to a good school to mix with other boys and further his education, so he sent him as a boarder to the well-known Westminster School in London. It did not take long for the tutors at this school to realize what a clever boy Christopher was. He seemed to have no difficulty with his lessons, and his progress was rapid.

Christopher had plenty of spare time at this school, and to make good use of it he began to take a great interest in science and astronomy. He soon found astronomy to be an absorbing hobby. It was fascinating to read all about the various stars in the heavens and then pick them out at nights. He began to experiment with telescopes and other instruments used by astronomers and made many geometrical drawings of the exact positions of the stars in the sky. He soon knew as much about the stars as many older and more experienced astronomers.

When he was thirteen he invented an astronomical instrument which he used to trace the paths of the stars through the sky. Although his instrument was never used by others, many great scientists who saw it praised Christopher highly for his skill in making it and could hardly believe that he had invented it himself.

During the next year (1646) his father moved him from Westminster School and sent him to Wadham College, Oxford, so that he might continue his education under the greatest professors in the country. Here he carried on his studies of science and astronomy, and it was not long before the professors had discovered what a remarkable youth he was. They were all amazed at his great knowledge and prophesied that he would one day become one of the greatest astronomers in the country. One day Christopher was discussing a problem with one of the professors when the latter said to him:

"Wren, you ought to attend the meetings of the Royal Society and hear the great scientists give their lectures. You would then have a far better opportunity of learning about all the new discoveries and inventions than you have now. It would help you greatly in your work."

30

Christopher replied:

"But surely I am too young, sir, to be admitted among such distinguished people? Although my father is a member, that does not give me the privilege of going to the meetings with him, dearly as I should love to."

The more Christopher thought about this talk, the greater was his desire to attend these meetings. He decided to ask his father to persuade the committee of the Royal Society to allow him to go to the meetings. At first his father told him to wait until he was older, but Christopher was so persistent that at last Dr Wren sought and gained the necessary permission. So Christopher began to attend the lectures with his father and was able to meet the most famous thinkers of the times. He had the gift of making friends with these clever people, and the scientists soon found him to be an interesting talker. So he had many scientific talks with famous people and in this way learned much more about his work than would have been possible otherwise.

It was not long before the great scientists came to realize the remarkable powers of this youth and found it enjoyable and instructive to listen to his conversation. Often he gave them valuable ideas and suggestions and occasionally took along an invention of his own to demonstrate before them. Among his inventions he made an improved set of lenses for a telescope, an instrument to demonstrate the motion of the earth, a weather clock, and a recording rain-gauge. He also assisted in the invention of the barometer.

Wren's name soon began to be talked about as a genius of science. Well-known people were using such phrases as "A youth of great inventive wit," "A rare and accomplished prodigy of science," and "An incomparable youth of science" when they discussed him to others. He was becoming famous as an astronomer.

By the time he was twenty-five, so great was the general opinion of his ability that he was appointed Professor of Astronomy at Gresham College in London. This was an exceedingly important post for one so young, but he carried out his duties so successfully that two years later he was appointed Professor of Astronomy at a more important college in Oxford. Here he had the opportunity of meeting many famous people who came, at various times, to look round the University.

So Wren now seemed set to spend the remainder of his life studying and lecturing about astronomy until such time as he should retire and be forgotten with the coming of the new and brilliant astronomers of the next generation to take his place.

But this was not to be, for the year 1661 brought a great turning-point in his life which was to make his name remain famous throughout history.

It happened in this way. During the past thirty-one years of Christopher's life King Charles I had been beheaded, Oliver Cromwell had come and gone, and now King Charles II was on the throne.

King Charles heard of the great genius of Wren from his courtiers and decided that such a brilliant man would be useful in his employ. So he sent to Christopher and commanded him to come and see him.

Wren was delighted to be honoured with a royal command and hastened to London immediately, trying to puzzle out why the King should wish to see him. But when he was shown into the King's chamber he was soon enlightened, for the King said:

"I have sent for you, Mr Wren, on the advice of certain of my courtiers. They inform me that you have a remarkable mind for solving all problems. If you are as brilliant as they would have me believe, you will be useful in my service. I am thinking of erecting a number of large

32

public buildings, and I have decided that you will be a useful assistant to my Surveyor-General, Sir John Denham."

Wren was dumbfounded. The Surveyor-General and his assistant were responsible for designing new buildings for the King, but he knew nothing about the art of building. He could not understand why the King had not given the work to an architect. Collecting his thoughts, he replied:

"It is a very great honour you confer upon me, your Majesty, but my knowledge of the art of the builder is little. I fear that I am unworthy of the position."

"Tut, tut," answered the King. "You have the ability to learn, have you not? It is my command. Go and acquaint yourself with Sir John Denham, who will help you with your new work."

So Wren went away, astounded that the King should have seen fit to appoint him to such a strange post. Nevertheless, he resolved to put all his energies into his new work and endeavour to learn all he could about the design and construction of buildings.

But he soon found that the work was not as difficult as he had imagined. His chief, Sir John Denham, was not a very good architect, being more fond of writing poetry than attending to his proper work, so Christopher found no difficulties in working under him.

For the first two years in his new job Wren spent most of his time drawing designs of buildings, and in this way he quickly learnt much about the art of building. Then in the year 1663 he had his first opportunity of testing his newly gained knowledge.

One day he went to dinner with his uncle, Dr Matthew Wren, who was, at that time, the President of Pembroke College, Cambridge. Dr Wren inquired of Christopher all about his new work and asked him if he thought himself capable of designing a building yet without aid.

Christopher replied:

"Yes, I am sure I could. In the past three years I have gained a fair knowledge of how to erect a good building, and I would like the opportunity of testing myself. But why do you ask?"

"Well, I recommended you to be the architect of the new chapel we are going to build at Pembroke College, and I have come to offer you the appointment. Do you think you can manage it?"

Wren was delighted with this offer. He now had the chance to design his first building, and he accepted the work eagerly.

It was not long before he set to work with vigour preparing his design for the chapel. He appointed builders to carry out the work and supervised them throughout the building's progress.

Less than two years later the chapel, a beautiful and imposing building, was finished. His first job as an architect stood up boldly for all to admire.

After he had started building Pembroke College Chapel, other people, seeing how good his work was, came to him with requests to build for them, and by the year 1665 he had, among many smaller jobs, built a theatre at Oxford, Trinity College at Cambridge, and a chapel at Emmanuel College, Cambridge. He was now beginning to make a name for himself as an architect.

In the same year a committee was appointed to examine the foundations of St Paul's Cathedral, London, which were badly in need of repair. Wren, Sir John Denham, and John Evelyn, the diarist, were the three most prominent members of this committee.

When Wren examined the walls and foundations of the church he found them to be in such a bad state that he advised the committee to build a new church instead of repairing the old one. But nobody would hear of this. It was far too expensive. Wren offered to prepare plans for a new church.

He had conceived an idea for a new and magnificent church with a great dome on the roof which should tower above London for all to admire. He prepared plans to show his idea and tried to convince the committee to accept them. But it was useless. They had decided to patch up the old church and would not listen to Wren's entreaties, saying that his scheme was a waste of time and money. Wren was extremely disappointed at having his plans turned down, for he had now set his heart on building a new St Paul's Cathedral.

To overcome his great disappointment he decided to take a holiday in France and visit the great buildings there and so add to his knowledge of architecture. He found much to interest him there, especially in Paris, where a great Italian architect was in the course of erecting one of France's most famous buildings, the Palace of the Louvre. He had many talks with this architect, picking up new ideas and fresh knowledge, and made many sketches of various buildings. In one letter which he wrote to his son during his stay in France he said:

I am learning much from examining and sketching the great buildings here. It is my business to pry into all trades and arts so that I may add to my knowledge.

In another he wrote:

I have busied myself in surveying the most esteemed buildings of Paris and the country around; the Louvre, for a while, was my daily object, where no less than a thousand men are employed building it; some in laying mighty foundations, some in raising stories, columns, etc., with vast stones by great and useful engines; others in carving, inlaying of marbles, painting, gilding, etc. which altogether makes a school of Architecture the best probably at this day in Europe.

Wren's daily visits to the Louvre stirred in his mind again the desire to carry out his plan to build a new St Paul's Cathedral. He wanted to make it the finest and most magnificent building in all England. Wondering if the committee had altered its opinion while he had been away, he returned to England to find out. Then an event happened which eventually gave Wren his great chance of realizing his ambition of building his great new St Paul's Cathedral.

The Great Fire of London took place. It started on a Sunday night in 1666 in a baker's shop near Fish Street Hill and raged through the narrow, choked streets of wooden houses, spreading rapidly westward across London. On, on it raged, burning to the ground everything in its path. It reached St Paul's and burnt that practically to the ground. By the time the Great Fire had finished its course of destruction it had destroyed more than thirteen thousand houses, fifty churches, and many other city buildings and hospitals.

The inhabitants of London were in a state of panic. Thousands of people were homeless. Something had to be done quickly. King Charles sent for Wren and ordered him to prepare plans for a new city. London had got to be rebuilt. It was a colossal task to give to one man, but Wren set about it with a great idea in his mind of designing this new London so magnificent and wonderful as to be beyond people's imagination. He realized that the Great Fire would not have been possible had the streets been wider and healthier and the tiny wooden houses less closely packed together. So he decided to make his new London a city of wide, straight, healthy streets free from all the old inconveniences and awkward narrow lanes and dark alleys.

He started his work by surveying the whole of the burnt-out area carefully and then set about the task of designing his new city. Here is an extract from his notes, showing clearly the brilliant idea that was in his mind:

> The streets to be of three Magnitudes, the three principal leading straight through the city and one or two cross streets to be at least ninety Feet wide; others sixty Feet and lanes about thirty Feet, excluding all narrow dark alleys without Thoroughfares and Courts. . . . The churches to be designed according to the best Forms of Capacity and Hearing adorned with useful Porticos and lofty ornamental Towers and Steeples.

Soon after Wren started preparing his plans the King issued a proclamation that no building must be started in London until the plans were finished. This was done to prevent private builders from hastily putting up shoddy houses in the old unhealthy manner.

But when Wren's plans were finished and shown to the people of London he had another great disappointment. They did not want his elaborate scheme. They preferred to live in their old unhealthy manner in narrow streets and tiny wooden houses rather than subject themselves to something they were not used to. Most of the objections to his plans came from the people who owned the land, for they were afraid that if the streets were made wider and the houses bigger they would be forced to give up some of their ground to make way for the new improvements. They wanted to build on the exact spots where their houses stood before they were burnt down. So great was the outcry against Wren and his ideas, and so urgent was the need for rebuilding to start, that the King had to give way to the people and allow them to rebuild in their own way. So London grew up again a city full of narrow, choked streets and unhealthy alleys, much to the distress and disappointment of Wren.

But Wren's other work went on unchecked, and he proceeded to design and rebuild many hospitals, churches, and other public buildings which had been destroyed by the Great Fire. The amount of work which he did at this period was enormous.

In 1669 the King was so delighted with the progress and beauty of Wren's work that he appointed him his

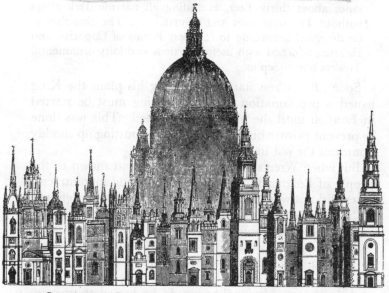

SOME OF THE PRINCIPAL TOWERS AND STEEPLES BUILT BY SIR CHRISTOPHER WREN (ST PAUL'S IS IN THE BACKGROUND)

Surveyor-General in place of Sir John Denham. Two other well-known architects of the time, Hugh May and John Webb, had each expected to be given this post, and they became very angry when they heard that Wren had got it. They thought it most unfair, as they had been leading architects all their lives and Wren had only spent nine years at the work. They did not appreciate the great work he had done in London since the Fire.

Then in 1673 the King bestowed the honour of a

knighthood on Wren for his services to London, and so he became Sir Christopher Wren.

By this time his plans for the new St Paul's had become valuable again. He was in charge of building London's new churches, and soon he would have to start doing something about the ruins of old St Paul's. But he

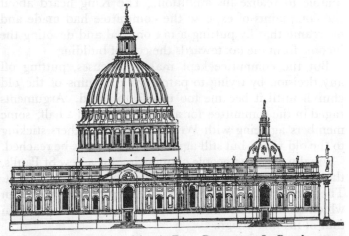

SIR CHRISTOPHER WREN'S FIRST DESIGN FOR ST PAUL'S

had to obtain the consent of the church committee before he could start the new building; so, to convince them of the worth of his design, he had an elaborate model of his proposed church made so that he could impress them with his scheme more clearly. This model is still preserved to-day in St Paul's Cathedral.

He showed the model to the committee and explained all its details, but some of the members would have nothing to do with it. They did not like its unusual design and thought it far better to rebuild the ruined church. Some of them said:

"Your building does not look like a church. Why has

it not got a steeple? The dome will be too heavy to hold up, and the place will collapse as soon as it is built. It will be much more sensible to rebuild the old church. We have not the money to spare for your extravagant design."

So Wren had to go away again still unsatisfied and unable to realize his ambition. The King heard about the complaints of expense the committee had made and overcame that by putting a tax on coal and devoting the income from the tax towards the cost of building.

But the committee kept making excuses, putting off any decision by trying to patch up the ruins of the old church until it became too unsafe to stand. Arguments raged in the committee for another year and a half, some members agreeing with Wren's ideas and others sticking to the old views, but still agreement could not be reached.

Finally, with the people clamouring for a new St Paul's, the committee were forced to do something about it. They reluctantly asked Wren to prepare a new design which would make the work of building less costly than that of his first design.

Sir Christopher prepared a new set of plans, laid them before the committee, and eagerly awaited their decision. After much discussion these plans were accepted on May 14, 1675, and Wren was given instructions to proceed with the erection of the building.

He was delighted. At last he had succeeded in his desire to build his magnificent church. It had taken him eleven years to get the committee to accept his proposals, and now he was satisfied. He was starting out on his greatest adventure in craftwork. Nothing so strikingly original in design as his St Paul's had ever been built in England before. He realized that he was taking a big risk with his design. The work of erecting a large building such as this was to be was, in those days, a

40

great feat of brains and skill. There were no cranes and machines to hoist the heavy stones and timbers to great heights, no steel girders to hold up the vast roof and to strengthen the walls, and no special steel scaffolds to make safe platforms for the workmen to stand on at heights. All sorts of ingenious ways had to be thought out to overcome these difficulties.

Even the foundations, it was feared by some, might not hold the stupendous weight of the walls, as the new building was to be quite different from its predecessor. But Wren was not afraid. He meant to succeed in this great work.

He carefully tested the soil on the site where the church was to be built, made numerous calculations, and then designed strong foundations.

Wren next searched for the finest craftsmen in the country to carry out the work from his plans. It was useless designing a beautiful building if he had poor craftsmen to build it. Wren meant to have the best obtainable. He appointed such famous craftsmen as Joshua Marshall, the stonemason, Charles Hopkins, the joiner, Richard Jennings, the carpenter, Jean Tijou, the decorative ironworker, and last but not least, that wonderful craftsman, Grinling Gibbons, to do the wood-carving. Each of these craftsmen employed a number of assistants to carry out their orders, for there was far more work to do in each craft than one man could possibly manage.

Wren also searched the country for suitable materials for the building, choosing the hard-wearing Portland stone for the walls and English oak for the woodwork.

Then everything was ready for the start, and Sir Christopher himself laid the first stone of the walls on June 21, 1675.

From that day on the work proceeded apace. Wren went every day to inspect the progress being made. When the walls had risen to a great height he used to have himself drawn up and lowered in a basket tied to a rope so that he might supervise the work of making the roof and the great dome.

The erection of the dome, which to-day still towers high over London to be seen for many miles around, was a marvellous feat of construction. It had to be built at such a great height over the vast opening between the walls that it looked an impossible task. But under Wren's expert guidance the craftsmen completed it successfully.

Actually the dome is composed of two separate domes, a low one which can be seen from inside the building surmounted by a tall one which serves as the roof. This was done to make the dome appear magnificent when viewed from both inside and outside the cathedral. Wren's brilliant mind foresaw that this would be necessary when he made his design for the dome, and he wanted it to look beautiful from whichever angle it was viewed.

So the work went on without interruption. The masons finished building the walls and columns supporting the roof, and then came the carpenters and joiners to lay the floors and make the oak seats and choir-stalls. Following them came Grinling Gibbons and his assistants to carry out their exquisite carvings, and finally Jean Tijou fixed up his beautifully forged wrought-iron screens and panels. Other craftsmen fitted the windows with glass and the seats with cushions, and expert painters completed the decorations.

Then, after thirty-five years' continual work, when Sir Christopher Wren had reached the age of seventy-eight, his great work was finished, in the year 1710, and the public were able to see the Cathedral in all its glory for the first time. Everybody abounded in their praise for the great architect. As they stood in the aisles or sat in the pews admiring the wonderful craftsmanship all round them they were all astounded with its magnificence. And in two hundred and fifty years opinions have not changed,

ST. PAUL'S CATHEDRAL
Photo: Will F. Taylor

for to-day St Paul's Cathedral is still considered to be one of the greatest masterpieces of architecture ever constructed.

During the years the work on the Cathedral was in progress Wren still continued to build churches all over

43

London. In all he designed and built over fifty churches in London, and it is a remarkable fact that every one was totally different in design from every other one. Some of his most famous parish churches still in use in London are St Bride's, Fleet Street, St Dunstan's-in-the-East, and

St Mary-le-Bow, Cheapside

A characteristic Wren steeple.

St Stephen's, Walbrook. It is part of the training of every modern architect to study the building of these churches so that they may learn from the example and genius of the great Sir Christopher Wren.

One of the most important public buildings which Wren built during his life was the Royal Observatory at Greenwich. This was erected in the year 1675 by order of the King so that observations of the weather might be taken and used to help British ships on their hazardous voyages into strange seas. This observatory is now used by countries in all parts of the world to obtain information about the weather conditions.

Another of Wren's great pieces of work was the Monument in London. At the time he was rebuilding London many people asked that some sort of monument should be erected to commemorate the Great Fire. Subscriptions were collected for the purpose, and Wren was asked to design it. But he saw a difficult task ahead. The people wanted it built near the scene of the outbreak of the fire; but looking round the narrow, dark streets which had risen again, he could not see how it was possible to design a monument to look imposing and effective in such a cramped space. The closely packed houses would obscure

44

it from view. What was he to do? The people wanted it, and he could not admit failure. Finally, after much thought, he hit upon the idea of building it in the form of a very tall column which would tower into the sky in stately fashion overshadowing all the dingy houses round it. So he designed his monument and built it in Fish Street a few yards away from the site of the baker's shop where the Fire started. The Monument, as it is now called, still stands and is another example of the skill and genius of this great architect. It is a great stone column, two hundred and two feet high, and enclosed in it is a marble staircase of three hundred and forty-five steps, up which visitors can climb to view London from the gallery at the top.

THE MONUMENT
Photo: Will F. Taylor

Among the enormous number of buildings which Wren designed and built during his long life, other well-known ones are the Chelsea Hospital, the Town Hall at Windsor, Temple Bar, which formerly stood in Fleet Street, and part of Hampton Court Palace.

But now that all this great work was accomplished, Sir Christopher was getting old and beginning to feel the need for more rest during his last years. So he began to devote more time to science and astronomy, the work of his younger days. and he gave many lectures to the Royal Society.

He also became a Member of Parliament after he had reached the age of eighty, but he still retained his position

45

of Surveyor-General to Queen Anne, who was now on the throne.

Unfortunately, though, he was not to hold that position for many more years, for when he was eighty-six a number of influential people at Court began to plot to relieve him of the post, as a friend of theirs wanted it. So they urged the Queen to dismiss Wren on the grounds that he was lazy and was not carrying out his duties properly. The Queen, thinking that they were speaking the truth, did as they asked and made the other man, who was an incompetent architect, her Surveyor-General.

Naturally this upset Sir Christopher terribly when he thought of all the great work he had done for London during his life, but he did not complain. All he said was: "They have only to walk round the streets of London to find out if I have been lazy. I am satisfied. My work will last for two hundred years, and future generations will be able to judge me."

All the great men of the country, though, did not turn from Wren. They admired him more than ever for the calm and dignified way in which he took this great rebuff from the Queen.

After this Sir Christopher retired to his home at Hampton Court to spend his few remaining years in peace. Once, each year, during this time he was taken back to the masterpiece of his creation, St Paul's Cathedral, so that he might sit inside for a while and recall pleasant memories of the time when he built it.

He died at his home on February 25, 1723, at the age of ninety-one, and was buried, fittingly enough, in St Paul's Cathedral. Over his tombstone there is now a tablet inscribed in Latin which says:

If you seek his monument, look round you.

III

GRINLING GIBBONS
Wood-carver

"GOODNESS, Beames, is it time for me to rise already? I hardly seem to have entered my bed since the Court

Banquet of last night," sighed John Evelyn as he languidly sat up in his expensively adorned four-poster bed in order to stretch his limbs and rub the sleepiness from his eyes.

Beames, his manservant, was in the act of flooding the imposing bedroom with daylight by drawing the heavy curtains away from the windows.

JOHN EVELYN

"Sir," he replied, "it is later than your usual time for rising, but I took the liberty of not disturbing you as you came in at such a late hour last night."

"Very wise of you, my thoughtful fellow, for a man cannot live without good and sufficient rest. But away with this slackness! I must start on my day. Hand

47

me my diary, so that I may record the events of yesterday."

Whatever John Evelyn might have failed to do in his daily tasks, the one thing he never forgot was to write his diary. He considered it most important that he should record the adventures and experiences of each day as it affected his life. He kept this diary very carefully for many years, right up to the day on which he died, and it contained so many closely written pages that when, many years later, it was published in book form, so that all might read it, it filled more than one thousand large printed pages.

And a very interesting book it is to read, too, because Evelyn, being a well-known and influential gentleman, was able to attend and write about all the most important functions of his time. He was a very great friend and companion to King Charles II and was always invited to the great banquets at the King's palace. In this way he met all the most famous people living in the country.

But let us get back to our story. The manservant laid the diary, together with quill and ink-horn, on the table at the bedside and left the room so that his master could write undisturbed. But Evelyn could not settle to his work. Last night's banquet had deadened his thinking-powers. His head ached and his eyes felt tired, so he decided to get dressed and take a sharp walk for an hour or so. Then he might feel more in the mood for it.

There was a cold nip in the January air as, half an hour later, Evelyn stepped from his stately home into the street.

"A glorious morning," he murmured to himself as he breathed in the clear air. "This should clear my brain and give me an appetite for lunch."

He strode off quickly down the cobbled street, undecided as to the direction he should take. After he had walked for about two miles, he thought it was time to return home, and so he cut across some fields to save time.

In one of the fields stood a ramshackle thatched cottage, and as he passed it he heard sounds of hammer-blows coming from within. Curiosity as to who should be working there bade him take a peep in the little latticed window. Imagine his surprise when he saw a young man, surrounded by chips and shavings, working away with chisel and mallet, carving a beautiful design in wood. The light through the window was not sufficient for Evelyn to distinguish the pattern on the wood, and he felt curious to know more about it. So he gave a tap on the window-pane with the knob of his stick and beckoned to the young fellow inside.

"May I come in to see your work?" he called.

"Why, surely you may enter, sir, if my abode is not too humble," came the prompt answer; "but I fear you may find a disappointment in my work."

The youth laid down his tools and went to the door to let Evelyn into the room. Evelyn's eyes immediately fell on the large piece of work on which the youth was engaged. He saw that it was a copy of a picture called *The Crucifixion*, painted by a great Italian painter many years before. Evelyn knew the picture well, as he had a copy of it hanging in his own home. But to see a copy of it here, in this tiny cottage, beautifully carved in wood, greatly astonished him. He wrote in his diary the next day about his visit, "I saw him doing such a work which for the skill of carving, drawing, and studious exactness, I have never before seen in all my travels."

"What a wonderful piece of work from one so young," said Evelyn in admiration. "But why do you work in such an obscure and lonesome place?"

The youth replied, "I am anxious to become a great

wood-carver some day, sir, and I find that I can apply myself more studiously to my work if I am not interrupted. But how did you find out where I lived, sir? No great gentleman has ever before honoured me with his presence here."

Evelyn did not answer his question but asked him to tell him about himself.

"My name, sir, is Grinling Gibbons, and I was born at Amsterdam, in Holland. I came over to England to pursue my craft of wood-carving, for which I felt I had some talent, so that I might better sell my work. I am now training myself so that I may one day offer my services to the great builders to carve their ornaments," answered the youth.

"Nonsense, young Gibbons," replied Evelyn. "To my eye your work is already that of a master craftsman. Look at those many carved figures of men. They are as perfect as hand can make them. And the frame is beautifully carved with fruit and flowers as delicate and tender as any natural ones."

Gibbons answered, "I thank you, honoured sir, for your kind praise, but I am yet a beginner and will do better with experience. Nevertheless, I should be glad to sell this piece of work to help me to carry on."

"That might easily be managed. But what is the price you are asking for it?" asked Evelyn.

Gibbons nervously pondered for a moment and then murmured, "Do you think one hundred pounds would be too great a price? I have put many hours of labour into it."

"Good gracious, no!" cried Evelyn. "Why, the frame alone is worth that, I'll be bound."

They discussed the best ways of selling the work, and eventually Evelyn suggested to the carver that he might be able to interest some great man in the work. Gibbons was delighted with this offer, and they went on talking about future jobs which might come his way.

After a while Evelyn got up to go, but he begged leave of Gibbons to visit him again in the near future.

When Evelyn had gone Gibbons set to wondering whom the great man might be who would want to see his work. He was extremely excited at the opportunity of showing his work to people who might give him further orders.

A few days after his visit to the carver's humble cottage, Evelyn went to the palace to dine with the King. During the meal Evelyn told the story of his finding the carver and begged the King to see his work.

"I have discovered a young carver, your Majesty, for whom I beg of you an audience," he said. "His work is of the most beautiful and delicate nature. He is also modest in his manner and agreeable in his accomplishments. Allow me to bring him and his work to Whitehall so that you may judge for yourself. I will stake my reputation with your Majesty that you have never seen any carving to approach it for quality. I predict that you will be exceedingly pleased and that you will employ him."

"Bring this unknown wonder along, Evelyn, and let me see if all you say is true," replied the King. "Why have I not been told of him before? No doubt I shall find him extremely useful."

Two days later, Evelyn, accompanied by two of his friends, Sir Christopher Wren and Mr Pepys, went along to the cottage in the field to tell Gibbons the good news.

The new visitors were shown the piece of carving which had pleased Evelyn on his previous visit, and they both expressed their admiration for it.

Evelyn then said to Gibbons, "You are commanded

to take this work to Whitehall to be viewed by his Majesty the King——"

"The King!" exclaimed Gibbons with feverish excitement. "This is indeed an honour far greater than I ever expected. I thank you for your kindness from the bottom of my heart."

After his visitors had gone, having left instructions for moving his work to Whitehall, Gibbons became in a great flurry at the thought of the ordeal before him. "How can a humble carver talk to such a great personage? I shall be tongue-tied. My knees will sag beneath me with nervousness," he thought.

Nevertheless, he carefully packed up his massive carved picture, slung it across his back, and set off for Whitehall. By the time he had arrived there he felt exhausted. The walk had been long and the carving heavy on his back, but these things had not deterred him. His eagerness to meet the King face to face was too great.

John Evelyn met him as appointed and took him to his father-in-law's chamber, which was situated in a part of the King's palace, for Sir Richard Browne was one of the King's ambassadors. Evelyn then went off to find the King and to tell him that Gibbons had arrived.

On being shown into the King's room, Evelyn said to him, "Your Majesty, the young wood-carver whom I mentioned to you some days ago has arrived, and he is awaiting your pleasure in my father-in-law's chamber. If it is the wish of your Majesty I will bring him and his work, although it is large and of heavy wood, to wherever you may appoint."

"No," said the King. "Show me the way, and I will go to Sir Richard's chamber"—which he immediately did, following Evelyn along the corridors of the great palace.

No sooner had he arrived in the room and cast his eyes

on the work than he was astonished at the excellence of it. Evelyn took Gibbons up to the King to kiss his hand, and the King began to talk to Gibbons about his work.

"Where did you learn your skill, young fellow?" he asked.

"In my humble room I have spent many hours with my tools cutting into wood, your Majesty, each time endeavouring to carve a better piece of work than the previous one. In this way I have hoped to become a skilful workman," replied Gibbons modestly.

"You have hoped to become a skilful worker?" repeated the King. "I am sure my friend Evelyn will agree that you are greatly skilled already. I offer you my compliments, young man. We must see what can be arranged about this picture. Let us take it to the Queen's chamber, so that she may give her judgment on it. Come, pick it up and follow me there."

The picture was set down in the Queen's chamber, where she and the King looked on and admired it. But just as the Queen was asking Gibbons the price he required for his work a message came in calling the King away on urgent State business. As he left the room he said to the Queen, "I must leave it to you to purchase this work and arrange with the carver for other employment."

The Queen turned to Gibbons again with the intention of telling him that she would purchase the picture when she was interrupted by one of the women in the room, a Frenchwoman by the name of Madame de Boord. This woman was a dealer in fancy petticoats, fans, and combs which she used to purchase in France and bring to England at regular intervals to sell to the great ladies of the land. The Queen and her ladies in waiting often made purchases from her. And this day she had been coaxing the Queen into buying an expensive fan just as the King had entered the chamber with Gibbons and his work. Seeing that the Queen was likely to buy the picture, which would mean she would not buy the fan, too, she said, with a note of jealousy in her voice:

"Do not be misled, your Majesty, into buying a worthless article. I am not so impressed by this so-called skilled work. Better work can be purchased in France at a much cheaper price. Regard the leaves and fruit in the frame. They are most carelessly executed. And the figures of the men—they are stiff and unreal. If you leave your purchasing for a time, your Majesty, I will find you a work which will please you."

And although this Madame de Boord knew nothing whatsoever about the goodness or badness of the carving, she was able to convince the Queen that it was unworthy of her attention. So she turned to the disappointed Gibbons and said:

"Take yourself and your base work away. I do not want it. Much better can I obtain elsewhere at a cheaper price."

So Gibbons, on the verge of tears at this abrupt dismissal, picked up his carving and staggered blindly from the room, followed by Evelyn.

When they arrived back at Sir Richard Browne's chamber Evelyn sympathized with Gibbons and promised to try to get his work bought by other great people. Evelyn was as disappointed as the carver.

So Gibbons packed up the picture again and, with a sad heart, dragged his burden back to his cottage at Deptford. A few weeks afterwards he sold the picture to Sir George Viner for a miserable eighty pounds.

The next day Evelyn went to see Gibbons again. He was in an angry mood because of his failure to make the Queen buy the carved picture and, thumping his fist on the carver's work-bench, he exclaimed, "If that disgust-

ing Frenchwoman had not been in the Queen's chamber
yesterday, your picture would have been sold and your
reputation as a great carver assured. But we must not
give up hope yet. I vow that sooner or later I will persuade the King to employ you. Meanwhile, we must find
others to give you work so that you may buy food and
materials for your craft."

So he continued to make great efforts to get his wealthy
acquaintances to recognize the skill of Gibbons and
brought many people to visit the carver's little cottage.
Two of the most famous of these visitors were Christopher
Wren, architect to the King, and Samuel Pepys, who had
much influence at Court. They spent quite a long time
watching Gibbons skilfully carve a portion of another
picture on which he was engaged, and then carefully
examined the various pieces of finished work lying about
the room. Evelyn hoped that Wren, who was in charge of
building many great churches and mansions, would be so
pleased with what he saw that he would employ Gibbons
to carve the woodwork in his buildings. But Wren was
not so ready to risk spoiling his beautiful buildings with
the carvings of this unknown man. He said that he already
had carvers in his employ and was not in need of any
more. Again Evelyn was astounded. Here was a young
man of greater skill than he had ever before seen, and yet
nobody seemed to want his work. He pleaded with
Wren to give him a trial; and after some discussion Wren
promised to do so when he could find some suitable work
for him. He said that he was then engaged on drawing
the plans for the new St Paul's Cathedral to take the place
of the old one, which had recently been burnt down in
the Great Fire of London, and he would see if he wanted
any extra carvers when he began building that.

Nevertheless, for all his disappointments, after a few
months the young carver obtained an order to carve the

woodwork in the mansion of a friend of Evelyn's named Christopher Bohun. Gibbons resolved to put the utmost of his skill into this work, so that friends of Mr Bohun might see it and desire that their houses should contain carving like it.

He carved the massive oak stairs, the panelling in the rooms, and the doors with beautiful festoons and sprays of fruit and flowers which were so skilfully executed that they looked real.

As Gibbons hoped, visitors to the house were enthusiastic about the marvellous work and began to ask him to decorate their houses similarly. Orders for carving-work began to pour in. Gibbons' name began to spread among famous and wealthy people. The carver was on the road to fame. Orders came in faster than he could work; people were grumbling because he was delaying their work. Finding that he must do something to satisfy his customers, he gave employment to two clever carvers from Holland. In order that their work should look as skilful as his when finished he drew all the designs for the carved panels and himself put the finishing touches to each man's work.

Evelyn was delighted that his carver should at last be recognized, but he still went about recommending him. Whenever Gibbons wanted more work, he would write to Evelyn and ask him to speak for him, as this letter shows:

JOHN EVELYN, ESQ.,

HONOURED SIR,

I would beg the faver when you see Sir Joseff William again you would be pleased to speak to him that he wold get me to carve his ladis sons house for I understand it will be very considerabell. If you have acquantance with my Lord to speak to him his self and I shall for ever be obliaged to you. I wold speack to Sir Josef my sealf but I know it would do better from you.

Sir, youre most umbell Sarvant,

G. GIBBONS.

London 23 Mar 1682

You will notice that Gibbons could not spell or write good English, but in those days there was no education for the ordinary kind of person. Only the sons and daughters of the very wealthy were taught to read and write properly.

One of the biggest mansions that Gibbons worked in during his early days of fame was known as Cassiobury Hall, the home of the Earl of Essex in Hertfordshire. There was so much work to do in this house that he had to employ more assistants. He also opened a workshop in London, where a number of assistants were kept continually busy. He also moved into London himself, taking a house near Ludgate Circus. It is said that, over the doorway of this house, he carved a panel which was so delicately executed that when the carriages of the wealthy passed by the leaves and flowers swayed naturally as though blowing in the wind.

When Gibbons had finished his work at Cassiobury Hall everybody was delighted with it. All the most famous people were praising the clever carver. Evelyn decided to take advantage of this by approaching the King again. He knew that his friend, Hugh May, was about to enter and rebuild parts of Windsor Castle, so Evelyn asked him to get the King's consent to employ Gibbons there. May, having seen and admired some of Gibbons' work, agreed.

So when he went to show the King his plans for the alterations he said, "There will be much wood to be carved, your Majesty, and I would suggest that you

57

employ one Grinling Gibbons, whose work is so exquisite that it surpasses that of any living man."

"Gibbons?" queried the King with a puzzled frown. "I have heard that name before.

"Ah, I remember," he went on after a pause. "He was the young fellow whom John Evelyn recommended

to me, and I viewed his picture. It certainly was an admirable piece of work for one so young. Yes, give him a trial if you feel that he will prove himself worthy of such employment."

So Evelyn had, at last, done what he had vowed to do. He had got the King to employ Gibbons.

All through the year 1677 joiners were busy at Windsor Castle making wainscots, doors,

GRINLING GIBBONS

and chimney-pieces ready for Gibbons to decorate them with carving. Early in the next year the carver and his assistants began work there. Gibbons spent most of his time drawing the designs and supervising his workmen. To make sure that the King would be pleased with the work, he did all the carving of the seats and choir-stalls in the King's chapel himself. The bill for its cost is still preserved in a museum, and it reads:

Carving work done and laid upon twenty eight seats and stalls. King's seat treated with great magnificence carved with six vases, thistles, roses and two boys besides laurels, palms, drapery, fruit, flowers and stars.

The cost of this work was £500, and it attracted great attention. Evelyn went to see it in 1683 and wrote in his diary:

> I went to Windsor to see the new work at Windsor chapel. I liked the stupendous, and beyond all description, incomparable carving of our Gibbons who is, without doubt, the greatest master both for invention and rareness of work that the world has ever had in any age.

The King was also highly delighted with Gibbons' work, and he appointed him to the coveted position of his Master Carver. This appointment assured Gibbons of certain fame, as he was now considered to be the greatest carver in England.

By this time he was employing numerous assistants to do his work, and he spent more time in carving in stone as well as in wood. In gratitude to Evelyn for putting him on the road to fame he carved a bust of his patron and presented it to him.

He also carved a life-size statue of the King, Charles II, which now stands at Chelsea, London, and sent to the King to come to his workshop to see and approve it.

The King was delighted with this figure, and Gibbons had a feeling of great pride. "I will show the King how really clever I am," he thought to himself.

So, pointing out a fault on the statue, he decided to show the King just how remarkable was his skill. Picking up a mallet and chisel, he went to strike at the faulty part. But he was nervous and struck too hard, breaking a piece which should not have been broken. The King laughed heartily at this and said, "That would not have happened but for your pride and impudent vanity. You cannot leave anything alone when it is all right."

Gibbons continued to carve for the rich and noble families. It became fashionable to have one's house adorned with a Grinling Gibbons' chimney-piece, clock-case, or panelled wall. So much work was carried out by himself and his assistants in the great mansions that there still remain many examples of his carving in various parts of the country.

By the year 1678, Gibbons was becoming quite wealthy, and he moved into a large house in Bow Street, Covent Garden. This house he decorated with his carvings and with many other works of art which interested him. When Evelyn visited him in 1679 he wrote in his diary:

> I went this morning to show the Duchess of Grafton the work of Mr Gibbons, the Carver, whom I first recommended to his Majesty. His house is furnished like a cabinet, not only with his own work, but with divers excellent paintings of the best hands.

It was in the year 1675 when Gibbons met Christopher Wren, the King's architect, for the second time. Wren called upon him to know if he would execute the carved work for St Paul's Cathedral, which he was just beginning to rebuild. He badly wanted the services of Gibbons to adorn his great buildings now, as he was the most famous wood-carver in the land, whereas before, when Evelyn had offered Gibbons to him, Wren had not bothered with him. But he had not then realized his cleverness.

The two men discussed the work and design of the new cathedral, and Wren said, "I am resolved to make this building the most beautiful in the land, and to do that I must employ the finest masons, carpenters, plasterers, and carvers it is possible to obtain. That is why I ask you to accept my offer. Your work can be surpassed by no man."

Gibbons had enough work on hand to keep him and his

numerous assistants busy for some years to come, so he was rather doubtful whether he would have time to do it. He wanted to do it, but it would not be fair to do that and disappoint others for whom he had promised to carve. He told Wren this, and the architect replied:

"It will take the masons some years yet to erect the walls and dome of the church, so you will have ample time to get your orders finished before it is ready for you. I plead with you. Do not refuse my request. I have set my heart on having my church adorned with your incomparable carvings."

After debating the matter for some time Gibbons decided to accept Wren's offer, on condition that he was allowed to use his own designs for the carvings. It was usual for the architect to instruct the carvers as to the designs they should carve, but Gibbons would have none of this. He wanted to create his own artistic ideas.

Wren did not object to this. He was delighted enough to know that Gibbons, the greatest of all carvers, had agreed to adorn his cathedral.

So the matter was settled, and Gibbons spent many spare hours in carefully drawing patterns for the seats and panels he was to carve when the building was ready.

It was not until 1694, nineteen years after Wren's visit, that the building was ready for Gibbons to start his work. Masons had been busy all these years erecting, stone by stone, the walls and dome, and the carpenters and joiners were finishing the choir-stalls and seats when Gibbons took his assistants along to begin the work which was to prove his greatest achievement.

Gibbons' first bill for work done was dated October 24, 1694, and read as follows:

Received then ye sume of fforty pounds in part payment for Carver's work done at St Paul's Church,

G. GIBBONS

61

Gibbons used mostly lime-wood for his carvings, as this bill of one of the joiners shows:

Work of a joiner in prepareing ye lime-tree for Mr Gibbons to carve for ye Choir at 3/- a day.

A vast amount of carving was executed all over the woodwork of the Cathedral, and one of the most notable examples, done by Gibbons himself, was the great organ-case, on which he modelled eight beautiful statues of angels. His bill for this read: "Charge about ye Great Organ Case for eight statue Angells at twenty pounds each."

When the work was completed and the Cathedral opened to the public, everybody was overwhelmed with wonder that human hands could execute such wonderful and exquisite carvings. Gibbons was hailed everywhere as the greatest carver ever known to man. And to-day his fame is still echoed throughout the world, although it is more than 200 years since he died. Visitors to London from abroad are always taken to St Paul's Cathedral to wonder at and admire this beautiful example of crafts-manship, which remains as unspoilt as when it was done.

After this success Gibbons worked with Wren in many other great buildings, the most notable being the King's palace at Hampton Court and the libraries of the Universities at Oxford and Cambridge.

Towards the end of his life the fashion for carved woodwork declined, but Gibbons retained the title of King's Master Carver until his death in January, 1721.

IV
JOHN HARRISON
Watch- and Clock-maker

JOHN HARRISON was born in the year 1693 at a village called Faulky, near Pontefract, Yorkshire.

His father, Henry Harrison, worked at the trade of carpenter and joiner on the country estate of a well-known gentleman of the time named Sir Rowland Winn. This gentleman occupied the position of the squire of the village of Faulky and lived in a large mansion called Nostell Priory, round which stretched over a large area the woods, fields, farms, and park-lands belonging to his estate.

JOHN HARRISON
From an engraving.

It was Mr Harrison's work to keep all the woodwork on this estate in good repair. There was always plenty of work to keep him busy, such as mending doors, fences, and gates of the various farm-houses and labourer's cottages belonging to his master. But in common with

63

all other workers in those days, his wages were very low and barely allowed his wife and himself enough to live on.

The birth of John caused Mr Harrison to look round for ways of earning additional money to buy the extra food now required. He had for some time been interested in the hobby of repairing clocks and watches, and he decided to ask his neighbours if he could see to any clocks and watches of theirs which wanted mending. In those days, nearly two hundred and fifty years ago, the kind of clocks that ordinary people could afford were far from being perfect in their mechanism and often went wrong. There was seldom a clock-repairer living within miles of a small village, and so the villagers often used their clocks more as ornaments than as timekeepers, owing to the difficulty of getting them repaired. For this reason Mr Harrison soon obtained plenty of repair-work, which he did in the evenings at home. It was not long before he was regularly occupied every evening on his new work.

At a very early age young John found it fascinating to watch the wheels and cogs in the mechanism of the clocks moving round. He would often spend his evenings sitting by his father at the kitchen table, watching with great interest his father's skilful fingers manipulating the tiny screws and wheels, as he took a clock mechanism to pieces to clean or repair it. He would pester his father incessantly with questions about the parts of each clock he was working at. He felt a great desire to know as much about clocks as his father.

When John was six years old he was unfortunate enough to fall ill with smallpox, which was then raging throughout the towns and villages of Yorkshire, and he had to stay in bed for several weeks.

Being a very active child, he found it very dull and monotonous lying in bed hour after hour, and after the first day he became very restless and fretful. He kept asking to get up, but his mother dared not let him for fear that it would do him harm. She tried all ways to amuse him, but with no avail. She sang to him and told him stories, but he was not interested. He wanted to get up. How he hated lying in bed!

By tea-time his mother was tired of trying to please him, and when Mr Harrison came home from work she said to him in a weary tone:

"John has been a worry to me to-day. I have tried everything I can think of to amuse him, but all he wants to do is to dress and come downstairs. I do not know how I shall manage to keep him in bed for several weeks, I am sure."

Mr Harrison answered that he would try to think of some way to amuse John. But it was not until after tea, when he was sitting down to his watch-repairing, that an idea struck him. He said to his wife:

"You know, I should not be surprised if John keeps asking to get up just so that he can watch me mending my clocks. He must be missing it greatly. I wonder if he would be happier if you gave him a watch to play with? I'll wind one up and open the back so that he can see the works moving. Give it to him in the morning, and see if it amuses him."

So the following morning Mrs Harrison laid the watch on John's pillow so that he could watch the moving cogs and wheels. Sure enough, as his father had guessed, John was delighted. Hour after hour he lay watching the cog-wheels, large and small, turning one another round. In his mind he traced the movement of the mechanism from the spring through the various cogs to the hands and soon gathered some idea of the principle on which the watch worked. His father was pleased that John had learnt so much about this watch all by himself. He said to him:

65

"When you are a little older I will let you help me repair the clocks and watches in the evenings, and I will teach you everything about them."

But things did not happen for Mr Harrison as he had expected, for when John was seven he came home from work one day and announced to his wife:

"Sir Rowland Winn has asked me to move to a new estate he has bought at Barrow-upon-Humber, in Lincolnshire. He wants me to be his head carpenter there."

This news was greeted in silence for a few moments. Mrs Harrison did not want to leave the village where she had lived all her life for a strange place, and John did not like the idea of leaving all his boy friends. After a while Mrs Harrison remarked:

"But if we move to this place you will lose your watch-repairing work, and we shall have less money to live on. I would rather stay here."

"Oh, you need not worry about money," replied the carpenter. "Sir Rowland is paying me higher wages this time, and I won't have to spend my evenings repairing clocks any more."

John then spoke up with a sorrowful note in his voice:

"But daddy! You promised to teach me how to repair watches, and I shall not be able to learn if you give that work up. I would rather stay here, too."

His father assured him that as soon as they had moved into their new home he would have plenty of time in which to teach John all he wanted to know. This satisfied the boy, and he did not mind leaving Faulky so much then.

After a time everything was settled, and the Harrisons moved to Barrow-upon-Humber.

Three years went by, and John was quite settled in his new surroundings. He had become a member of the church choir and had made friends with other boys there. On weekdays, as there were no schools to attend, he spent most of his time in his father's workshop tinkering at old clocks and any old pieces of machinery which contained moving wheels. He never seemed to tire of playing with wheels and cogs; his father had kept his word and taught him much about watch-repairing, so that he had now a good knowledge of the work.

The vicar of the church which John attended was a learned and kindly gentleman, and he offered to teach any of the choir-boys who desired it to learn to read, write, and calculate. John was one of the boys who accepted this opportunity, and he started to have lessons at the vicarage.

Although he quickly showed ability with figures, being able to measure and calculate very easily, he was not very successful with his reading and writing. He did not seem to be able to learn these subjects at all, and the vicar lent him a book to try to help him. He said as he handed John the book:

"Here is a book that tells you all about clocks and watches. As you are so interested in them, it might help your reading. Take it home, and try to read it through."

John thanked the vicar, but when he had reached home and started to try to read the book he found that the drawings of the clock-mechanisms took his attention so that he could not give his mind to the words. Finally, instead of pursuing the difficult task of trying to read, he started carefully copying out all the diagrams in the book. This did not help his reading, of course, but it taught him much more about his hobby of studying clocks and watches.

Two years later John was old enough to start work, and he began to learn the trade of carpenter and joiner under his father. He enjoyed this work and soon became very skilful at using the planes, chisels, saws, and other carpenter's tools.

By the time John was fifteen he was able to earn a little extra money by measuring and surveying land for farmers in the evenings, but whenever he had an evening to spare he would go to the workshop and carry on his experiments with clocks. Besides repairing them, he was always trying to discover ways of improving their construction so that they would keep time better. He was always making new parts and trying them in the clocks.

JOHN HARRISON'S CLOCK, 1715
All the wheels are of wood except the escapement.
From an exhibit in the Science Museum, South Kensington

Eventually, in the year 1715, when he was eighteen, he successfully constructed a complete eight-day clock, making all the cog-wheels of wood. Many hours he must have spent and many disappointments he must have suffered in trying to carve the teeth accurately on such tiny wheels. But his determination to succeed was great. So well did he make this clock that it is still in going order in the Science Museum in London.

Although delighted to have succeeded in constructing

such a good clock, John did not rest there. He carried on his experiments as before. He tried to discover why the clocks of those days always lost time in the summer and gained in the winter. He eventually found that this was caused by the expansion and contraction of the metal pendulum according to the temperature, but he could not see for a long time how to overcome this trouble. He tried all kinds of devices without success, until the year 1726, when he invented what was afterwards known as 'Harrison's gridiron pendulum.'

Instead of making it from one piece of metal, as previously, John made his pendulum from a number of parallel alternate rods of brass and steel and suspended the bob of the pendulum from them. He so arranged it that the downward expansion of the steel rods was exactly compensated for by the upward expansion of the brass ones, and so kept the pendulum swinging evenly all the year round. This principle for the pendulum is still generally in use to-day and is known as the 'compensating pendulum.'

After this success John gave up his work as carpenter and joiner and devoted his whole time to making and experimenting with clocks and watches. One of the first eight-day clocks he made containing his 'gridiron pendulum' is still in working order in the museum of the Company of Clock-makers in the Guildhall, London.

John went on making improvement after improvement in the mechanism of clocks, and his business continually increased accordingly. Harrison's watches and clocks were beginning to become well known, and many people sought after them.

But his ambitions were now turning towards another and more profitable goal. Some years previously, in 1713, an Act was passed in Parliament offering prizes of £10,000, £15,000, and £20,000 to anyone who could invent and construct an instrument which would measure

E

the position of a ship at sea accurately to within a distance of sixty, forty, and thirty geographical miles respectively. The Government was anxious, at the time, to do something to help the English ships make their hazardous voyages into unknown seas with less risk of being lost or delayed. It was thought that if a clock could be invented which would keep accurate time despite the motion of the ship, the sailors would be better able to calculate their position on the sea.

A committee called the Board of Longitude had been formed to judge the entries in the competition, but no inventors had, up to the year 1726, managed to make an instrument suitable for the purpose.

John Harrison heard of the competition and the enormous prizes offered and thought that he could construct a clock such as the Board of Longitude desired. So he set to work and experimented. For two years he struggled on, suffering many disappointments and failures. Often, just as he thought he had succeeded in his task, he would find something unsuitable in his design and have to start all over again. But he was rewarded for his determination and skill at last. He constructed a clock which he found to be quite satisfactory. He made careful detailed drawings of it and went off to London to claim his prize from the Board of Longitude.

He first went to see a gentleman by the name of George Graham, and he showed him his drawings. Graham made a careful study of them and then said to Harrison:

"From what I can understand of these diagrams I should say that you have easily succeeded in inventing an instrument excellent enough to earn the Board of Longitude's prize money. But let me advise you. I should not take these drawings along to the Board and expect to draw your money. They will want to see a workable instrument first. If I were you, I should go back home and construct a faultless example of your instrument. Then you can show it to the Board together with the drawings."

John took his advice and returned home. He was now the father of a grown son named William, who helped him in his business. He had learnt to be a watch- and clockmaker from his father. So father and son started together making their ship's clock, which was to be good enough to claim the prize money. Whenever they found an opportunity they toiled at it, making each tiny part of the mechanism with great care and accuracy. Nevertheless, the ordinary business of making clocks and watches had to be carried on, too, so father and son did not get nearly so much time to work at the instrument as they would have liked.

It was not until the beginning of the year 1735 that the clock was finished to Harrison's satisfaction. He was now certain that it was as nearly perfect as he could make it. It was certainly a wonderful instrument, judged by the standards of those days. Every tooth on every cog fitted into its fellow perfectly, and every spindle was perfectly balanced. The complete instrument was so poised that if it was fixed up in a ship it would remain horizontal and steady, whatever inclination the ship took in rough seas and stormy weather. In this way Harrison hoped to make his clock keep perfect time.

As soon as it was completed John Harrison packed it up carefully and took it to London to show to Mr Graham.

Graham saw it and asked if he could keep it for a few days to test it. When he next saw John he told him:

"It is a fine instrument and well worthy of at least part of the prize money you are aiming at getting. I will give you a certificate of its excellence. But before you show it to the Board of Longitude it would be advisable to test it thoroughly on a ship's voyage, so that you may have some facts about its accuracy to place before them.

For if you show it to them now they will perhaps refuse you any share of the prize on the grounds that you cannot prove its worth and that you have not tried it on a ship."

"With my business needing attention I cannot really spare the time to go away for a voyage long enough to test the instrument properly, I fear. It looks as though I

FIRST MARINE CHRONOMETER MADE BY JOHN HARRISON
National Maritime Museum, Greenwich

shall have to give up the idea of ever trying for that prize," replied Harrison despondently.

"Of course you must not do that," said Graham emphatically. "You cannot leave your instrument to rot, now that you have brought it to such a state of perfection. Why not leave your son, William, to look after the business while you are gone on the voyage?"

Harrison did not like the idea, but after much persuasion from Graham he agreed to do as asked. A few weeks later he was aboard a ship bound for Lisbon with his chronometer, as he had named his instrument, fixed up for testing in the captain's cabin.

Many times a day during the voyage would he go to his chronometer and make calculations from it. His anxiety was great. He was afraid that the instrument would fail in its purpose through some unforeseen fault in its mechanism. But he need not have feared, for on the way home he succeeded, by means of his chronometer, in correcting the direction the ship was taking by one and a half degrees.

Harrison was now ready to show his instrument to the Board of Longitude and claim part of the prize, for his success was not sufficient for him to expect all the prize money. He hoped to improve his instrument when he got home sufficiently to claim that.

But however little of the prize money he expected to receive, he had not counted on the meanness which the Board of Longitude showed towards him.

When he arrived back in London he took his chronometer together with the drawings of it to George Graham, explained his success on the voyage, and asked him to put his invention before the Board of Longitude for their opinion of it.

When he next went to see Graham, the latter said:

"I am afraid I have bad news for you. The Board studied your chronometer, but they were not satisfied with your claims as to its accuracy. They agreed, though, that it was a better instrument than any they had seen before and have decided to offer you a prize of five hundred pounds for it. I told them that it was worth at least a thousand pounds, but it was of no avail. They seem to want to keep the prize money, so I fear you will have to be satisfied with what they offer you."

Harrison replied:

"I thank you for your assistance, but five hundred pounds is little enough return for all the work I have done in inventing and making this chronometer. Nevertheless,

I am resolved to get that prize some day. I will use this money to make a better instrument."

So with grim determination Harrison went back home and set to work on his second chronometer. He made it much smaller and less clumsy than the previous one and had it completed in the year 1739. But the Board of Longitude again refused to give him even a part of the prize money. They still made excuses about its accuracy. They also doubted John's statement about its performance, saying that it sounded too good to be true.

Naturally John was very angry, but his great determination to prove the worth of his instrument did not waver. He said to William with a tone of strong conviction in his voice:

"I will work to make the Board of Longitude pay me my rightful prize money, even if it takes me the rest of my life to do it. I will not give in to them now that I have succeeded so far."

So again he set to work on a third chronometer, but his ordinary clock-making business was now so flourishing that he had little time to spare for his experiments. However, whenever he found himself free for a few hours, he would do a little towards it. Slowly the work went forward, and it was not until the year 1749 that he had it finished and ready to demonstrate to the Board of Longitude. He first showed it to that famous body of scientists the Royal Society, so that they might pass a fair judgment on its merits. As soon as they had tested it, these scientists praised it highly, saying that no timekeeper had ever been made so accurately before. So excellent did they consider this chronometer that they awarded Harrison a Gold Medal for his skilful workmanship.

Now that the Royal Society had shown its favour towards John's third chronometer, surely the Board of Longitude would be forced to recognize its value and accuracy? But it was not to be! They continued to side-step Harrison's claims. John tried all the means in his power to make them change their minds. The weeks lengthened into months, and still John was no nearer to his goal. Any other man, with less determination than John Harrison, would have long ago given up his efforts in despair after so many disappointments. But he started again and began to construct a fourth chronometer!

This instrument he made greatly superior to any of the previous ones. At each fresh attempt he found means of introducing new improvements to the works. This time the instrument was made much smaller, being only five inches across the face and rather like a large pocket-watch in appearance. John was certain that this one would work accurately enough to satisfy the Board's requirements for being capable of determining a ship's position at sea within a dis-

JOHN HARRISON'S FOURTH CHRONOMETER, 1759

From the original in the Science Museum, South Kensington, London

tance of sixty geographical miles. Nevertheless, to be absolutely certain of his claim he meant to test it thoroughly before showing it to the Board.

He said to his son William:

"I want you to take the chronometer on a voyage to test it as I did the first one we made. But your trip must be of longer duration than mine was, so that the instrument can have a thorough testing. I am arranging for you to go to Jamaica and back on board a merchant ship.

"I shall expect you to make very careful observations daily of the working of the instrument, and you must bring back the exact information of any errors you may find in it. I am confident that this time we shall be able to show the Board of Longitude remarkable evidence of its accurate timekeeping."

So the voyage was arranged, and on November 18, 1761, William Harrison set sail from Portsmouth for Jamaica in the West Indies. The voyage lasted throughout the winter, and all that time John Harrison waited anxiously at home for the important news of the success or failure of his new chronometer.

The months passed very slowly for John, but eventually he received word that the ship carrying his son was due in at Portsmouth harbour on March 26, 1762. He journeyed down there to meet the ship.

He could scarcely control his excitement as he ran to greet William. What would he have to tell him? Would the news be good or bad? He expected it to be good, knowing how accurately he had made the instrument; but he dared not be too confident about it, in case something had gone wrong.

But as soon as William noticed his father coming towards him a happy smile broke out on his face. He waved and began to shout excitedly:

"The chronometer has acted perfectly, father! The voyage has been a success! Congratulations!"

As soon as they had embraced each other, Mr Harrison was anxious to hear the full news. He asked:

"Tell me what errors it made in the timing. Have you collected any useful figures to show to the Board?"

William replied quickly:

"No need to worry about the Board now, father. They will have to pay us the prize money whether they like it or not. For the whole five months I have been on the ship the chronometer has erred no more than one minute fifty-four and a half seconds from the correct time. I

76

think that is marvellous! Nobody could ever hope to make a more accurate timekeeper than that."

Mr Harrison quickly made a few calculations in his head and then exclaimed:

"Why, it is even better than I had dared to hope! The slight error it has made means that it is capable of measuring a ship's position on the sea to within eighteen geographical miles, and to obtain the Board's highest prize of £20,000 it only need be accurate to within thirty miles. So we are bound to receive the money now. They will be unable to refuse us it."

But unfortunately John's expectations were not to be fulfilled so easily as he had hoped. Again the Board of Longitude held back his money when John went to claim it. Time after time they made various weak excuses for not certifying his right to the prize. John tried all manner of ways to get them to give him his reward, but without success.

Eventually, angry and exasperated, John petitioned Parliament and asked them to make the Board pay him. Parliament carefully considered his claims and thought that he was entitled to at least a portion of the prize money. So an Act was passed authorizing him to receive a quarter of the reward, which amounted to £5000. Surely the Board would have to satisfy Harrison's claims now that Parliament ordered them to? But although it sounds incredible, they escaped their obligations by giving him a small sum on account and promising to pay him the remainder at an early date.

Naturally John was dumbfounded at the Board's refusal this time. He knew that he would never get the money now that the Board had only promised him it. He had become used to their idle promises, which were given without any intention of keeping them. And if the Board took such little notice of an Act of Parliament as to ignore it, there was no way at all to make them keep their promise.

Thoroughly disheartened at the ungratefulness shown to him after his many years of work for the benefit of shipping, he decided that the only thing left for him to do was to go back to his work and try to forget the shameful treatment he had received. But he soon found that he could not leave his chronometer alone. It had become part of his existence now. He was always wanting to try to improve it. He started to take it apart to see if he could find any faults with the mechanism. He made various small alterations which he thought would increase its accuracy as a timekeeper. Eventually he got it working so well that he said to his son William:

"I want you to take the chronometer on another sea-voyage. I think you might find an improvement in its performance over that of last time."

"But it is impossible to improve it much, father. And what is the use of my going, anyway? Even if it is better than before, we shall get nothing for it. The Board of Longitude will still find a reason to say that it is unworthy of their prize."

Nevertheless, Mr Harrison wanted to test the instrument again for his own satisfaction, and so William set sail again for the West Indies on March 28, 1764. The four months' voyage across the Atlantic Ocean and back was marked by many spells of rough weather and stormy seas. It was the kind of weather to cause any chronometer but the very best to fail in its duty. But Harrison's instrument worked admirably all the time, and on arriving home William informed his father it had kept its time so accurately that it had been possible to calculate the ship's position at sea to within ten geographical miles —one-third of the distance required to gain the Board's prize!

Harrison then wrote to the Board of Longitude and to Parliament and informed them of this fresh success of his instrument and again sent in a claim for the prize.

But still the Board withheld their certificate and prize money, although they admitted that Harrison's claims for his instrument entitled him to the reward.

They made the excuse that they had no proof that his claims were correct. They also made the suggestion that the statements of his son and the captain of the ship on which the chronometer was tested were false.

Parliament was not so suspicious of Harrison's honesty, though, but they saw the need to satisfy the Board of Longitude as to the instrument's efficiency. So they passed a new Act awarding Harrison the payment of a sum of money which, together with what he had already received, would amount to half the prize money. The Act also gave certain conditions which must be carried out before the money could be claimed. These conditions stated that a copy of the chronometer must be made by another clock-maker and then tested on a ship's voyage.

When Harrison heard of the terms of the Act he said to his son:

"So they still think that I am a fraud. Well, let them carry out their conditions, and if they can find a clock-maker skilful enough to construct the instrument I shall be sure to get the reward at last."

On August 22, 1765, Harrison went to London and explained the construction of his instrument to the Astronomer Royal and six expert clock-makers. He then handed detailed drawings of the mechanism to a clock-maker named Larcum Kendall, who was appointed to make the duplicate instrument.

When Kendall had finished his copy it was tested for accuracy by Harrison and then fixed on the ship which was to take Captain Cook on his famous voyage round the world.

Many months later Cook returned from his voyage and announced to the Board of Longitude that he had proved Harrison's claims of the chronometer to be correct. The instrument had been remarkably accurate at all times during the voyage.

Even after this proof the Board of Longitude held back the prize money by continuing to make many more frivolous trials with the timekeeper.

So exasperated and impatient did John become that he appealed to the King and asked him to force the Board to give up the prize. The King replied and ordered him to erect one of his chronometers in the Royal Observatory at Richmond, where he would test it himself. John carried out the King's bidding, and after ten weeks' trial his Majesty found that the instrument had erred by less than four and a half seconds during the whole of that time. He was satisfied that the prize money had been earned by Harrison, and he made an order for it to be given to him at once.

So after a lifetime of struggling for his rights, John received his money at last.

The four chronometers which Harrison spent so many years in constructing are still preserved in the Royal Observatory at Greenwich.

The success which eventually came to John made his name famous throughout the country, and he was nicknamed 'Longitude Harrison.' Although his name is not remembered by many people to-day, modern shipping still owes much to the skill and craftsmanship of John Harrison, for one of the most important instruments on any ship is its chronometer.

John Harrison lived to the age of eighty-three and died in Red Lion Square, London, on March 24, 1776.

V

THOMAS CHIPPENDALE

Cabinet-maker

DURING the early eighteenth century there was living, in the tiny village of Otley, in Yorkshire, a man by the name of John Chippendale. His house was one of the small thatched cottages which overlooked the village green. Adjoining the cottage was a little workshop where he carried on the trade of carpenter and joiner. Whenever any villager or farmer needed a new stool or table, fence or gate, Mr Chippendale was the man who made it from the tough oaken boards which he hewed from timber taken from the trees in the neighbourhood.

He was a good craftsman and greatly respected by all the villagers. They knew that if they bought any wooden article from Mr Chippendale it would be strong enough to last a life-time. The squire of the village also used to keep the carpenter busy repairing woodwork on his estate, and often used to ride up to the little workshop to give an order and have a friendly chat with him.

The workshop was a small room containing a long wooden bench which stood against the back wall of the room. A vice was clamped on one end of the bench, so that Mr Chippendale could hold his wood firmly while. he planed and chiselled it into a chair or table-leg or part of some other piece of solid furniture. A number of planks and boards of oak stood against the walls ready for use when needed, and a shelf above the bench displayed a rather untidy assortment of boxes containing screws, nails, glue, iron hinges, latches, and other small sundries necessary for his work. There

81

were racks filled with assorted chisels and gouges; saws
of various shapes hung from nails driven into the wall
and queer-looking planes lay on the bench. The floor
was covered with an abundance of wood-shavings. Mr
Chippendale did not often sweep them up, as they helped
to keep his feet warm in cold weather; only when it
became difficult to walk in them would he gather them
up and take them into the garden at the back to burn them.

Mr Chippendale's days at the bench were long and
arduous. He would invariably start his work at six
o'clock in the morning and carry on until seven or eight
o'clock in the evening, only pausing for short periods to
have his meals. During the evenings when the daylight
had gone he would work by the aid of tallow candles,
fixed in brackets on the wall, as there was neither gas,
electric light, nor oil-lamps in those days.

But for all the long and tiring hours Mr Chippendale
had to work each day, he loved his job. He never got
tired of making things with his skilful hands, and he lived
a very happy life.

Mr Chippendale was the father of a five-year-old son,
named Thomas, born in the year 1718. The carpenter
was very fond of his son and longed for the day when he
would be old enough to be taken into the workshop to
learn the craft of woodworking. There were many jobs
he found difficult to do by himself, and when Thomas
grew up he would be a great help to him.

When the carpenter was working at his bench he could
see out on to the village green, shaded by two great
chestnut trees, through a tiny window which gave the
only light to his workshop. Often he would stop in his
work for a few moments to rest and watch the antics of
Thomas as he played under the trees with the other
children of the village.

One day he glanced out of the window to see why the

children had suddenly stopped their screaming and chattering. Looking through his window, he noticed that the squire had just ridden in on his horse, followed by four of his serving-men. He saw the children make a respectful salute as the squire came near, and then he noticed that the squire had beckoned Thomas over to him. They began talking, so the carpenter, wondering idly what the squire had to say to his boy, turned from the window and resumed his interrupted work.

He had not long to wait, though, to know the reason for the squire's talk with his son, for a few moments later, Thomas came running into the workshop with his face wreathed in smiles.

Holding out his hand, he said excitedly:

"Look, father, the squire has given me a farthing."

"You are a lucky boy, to be sure," said the carpenter. "But what did he give you it for? Did he want you to do something for him?"

"Yes, he said that he was in a hurry and had not time to call on you, so he told me to tell you that the gate in his twelve-acre field needs mending as soon as you can do it. He gave me the money for bringing the message to you," replied Thomas.

"All right, son, I will see to the gate to-morrow if the weather holds fine," said Mr Chippendale as he resumed his work after this second interruption.

Thomas did not leave the workshop to go back to play on the green, though. He stood, idly kicking the shavings about with his foot, and with a very thoughtful look on his face. After a few moments he looked up at his father and asked abruptly:

"Father! Where is London?"

"London? Why, that is a big city many miles from here. But what makes you ask me that?" queried his father with a puzzled look on his face.

"The squire told me that he was making a journey to London and said that he would be away for more than a month. I wondered what sort of a place it could be for the squire to want to go there," replied Thomas.

It may seem strange to us that Thomas had never heard of London; but living in a little country village in those days was vastly different from what it is to-day. There were no trains or motor-cars, not many newspapers or books, and few were the travellers who came to the villages to spread the news of happenings in other parts. So children seldom saw or heard anything of things and places outside their own village. They had no schools to go to, and most of their time was spent in playing in the fields near their homes.

Even Mr Chippendale himself had never travelled farther from his home than to the neighbouring villages, but he had often spent an evening in the local hostelry supping his ale while he listened to the tales of a traveller who was putting up there for the night. In this way he had heard things about London and other far-distant places.

He said to Thomas, who was waiting to hear some more about the place to which the squire was journeying:

"Yes, child, I have heard from the travellers that London is a fine city full of grand streets of houses, every one as big as our squire's manor-house. Many fine ladies and gentlemen live in these houses, and they say that London is the place where all the great lords and ladies of the land live in the winter. Our King, too, lives in a great palace there, which is said to have as many rooms in it as there are in all the houses in Otley put together."

"It must be a wonderful place," remarked Thomas. He seemed to be very interested in this great city, and after a few moments he asked his father:

84

"Do carpenters live in London, too, father?" To which the carpenter replied:

"Of course they do, child, or how do you think the folk who live in the great houses get their chairs and tables made and mended? They say that there are many very skilful makers of cabinets and other things of wood. There they make chairs with beautiful carvings on them, taking much time to make and costing many pounds to buy. But run along now, child, and play. I have my work to do, and little time to spare to tell you stories. I will tell you more about London some other time."

So Thomas went out of the workshop—but not to play. He squatted down on the path with his back resting against the wall and began to think:

"It would be grand to live in London. When I grow up into a man I'll go there. If I learn to be a clever carpenter like father and save the money that the squire gives me, I shall be able to buy a big horse and ride there. Then I'll mend the chairs and tables for the rich people and earn a lot of money. So I might become a rich man."

Thomas could think of nothing but London for weeks after. It seemed like a beautiful dreamland to him, full of rich people and grand streets and houses. He made up his childish mind that he must go there and see all these wonderful things his father had told him about.

He decided to be bold enough when next the squire spoke to him and ask him more about the wonders of London. He did not have long to wait. About three days after his return to Otley the squire came into the workshop to see Mr Chippendale about some repairs he wanted done at the manor.

Thomas, luckily for him, was in the workshop at the time, for he had just brought in his father's lunch of a jug of ale and bread and cheese. He seized his chance to

F

speak to the squire just as he was leaving, and, although he felt extremely nervous, he said:

"Please, sir, do carpenters live in London?"

The squire looked astonished at first. This seemed a queer sort of question from a child. But, with a smile breaking upon his lips, he replied:

"Why, of course they do, boy, just as in any other town or village, or how could people get their houses built and their furniture made? What a funny question to ask me! Tell me what put it into your mind."

"Well, sir, father told me what a wonderful place London was, and when I am a man I am going there to work," replied Thomas seriously.

The squire laughed again and said:

"You are very young to start thinking about what you will do when you are a man; but learn all you can about your craft from your father, and then we shall see what can be done for you when you are older. But you will have forgotten all about it by then."

Thomas meekly thanked the squire as he left the workshop for his kind words, and sat down to dream again about the time when he would be able to go to the great city.

Weeks passed into years, and eventually Thomas started helping his father at the work-bench. He quickly learned how to handle the tools, and it was not long before he could do many carpentering-jobs all by himself. His father began to send him out to do little jobs such as repairing gates, fences, and such-like things, and he felt very proud of his father's trust in him. He took every opportunity he could to learn more about his work. He was still convinced that as soon as he had become a clever workman he would go to London.

Through this great interest he learned the craft of wood-working so quickly that by the age of sixteen he could make a solid oak table or chair quite as skilfully as his father.

Now that he was older he was able to do as other youths and men of the village, and spend his evenings in the local hostelry talking and playing games. Whenever he heard that a traveller was staying in the village overnight he would hurry down to the hostelry as soon as his day's work was over to listen to the traveller's tales, in the hope that he would pick up some fresh knowledge about London and the ways of the people living there.

By this time his father was paying him a small wage for his work, and Thomas was careful not to spend it. He hid it away, week by week, in a little wooden box he had made, ready for the day when he would have enough to take him to London.

When he was nineteen he had saved up enough to buy a horse; so he decided that it was now time for him to make that journey to London about which he had dreamed ever since the squire had spoken to him when he was five years old.

When he had made all his plans he told his father of his intentions.

"Father, you will, no doubt, be surprised and disappointed in me for what I am going to do, but I have decided to leave Otley and make the journey to London, for which I have been saving my money for years. I have enough money to buy a horse and pay for my lodging on the way, and ——"

But his father, overcoming his astonishment, interrupted him and cried:

"Goodness, son! Surely you are joking? You cannot think of doing such a silly thing. How can you leave home after I have brought you up and taught you your craft, just to waste your savings on such a foolhardy journey? Who will look after the workshop when I am dead if you leave the village? And how do you know that the smart cabinet-makers in London will want to give work to you, a country carpenter? Get the silly idea out of your head, son, and get on with your work. The squire wants some jobs done at the manor this morning, so get your tools packed and be off with you."

Mr Chippendale could not really believe that Thomas had meant what he had said. He fully expected to see him do as he was bid and pack up his tools to go to the squire's. But no, Thomas was in earnest. He did not mean to be put off. He had made up his mind to go to London, and to London would he go, however much it hurt him to leave his home and village. So he answered:

"I am sorry, Father, but for years I have been preparing for this journey, and now that I am ready I must go. If I am unlucky when I reach London I will come back and trust that you may give me work again. I shall not complain if once I have seen and walked along the streets of London."

The carpenter now came to realize that his son was determined to go, so he decided that it would be useless to try to keep him at home.

So, although extremely disappointed in his son, Mr Chippendale gave Thomas a bag of tools for his trade and went with him to a local farmer to buy a horse.

Two days later Thomas started on his journey. After many sad farewells from his parents, Thomas leapt astride his horse and went off in a canter down the street. His parents watched him out of sight and returned sorrowfully into their cottage. Great was their grief at losing their son, and they prayed that no ill should befall him on the way.

As soon as Thomas had left the village, his spirits rose. He was on the way to his dreamland at last! In four or five days he would be looking for lodgings in the great city. How thrilling it all was to him!

He spurred his horse on, so anxious was he to make the journey as fast as possible. He rode all day, only giving his horse an occasional rest for a drink at a stream, until at sunset he put up at a village hostelry for the night. He could not sleep, however; his anxiety to finish the journey was too great. As soon as dawn broke he was up and off on the next stage of his journey.

Again he rode hour after hour, but unknowingly he was working his horse too hard. It began to drag and falter. Then suddenly it tripped in a pot-hole in the road and fell heavily on its neck. Luckily for Thomas he was thrown into the long grass at the side and was only shocked and stunned for a few moments.

He rose and went to help his horse up again but, catching his breath, saw that it was too late. His horse was dead.

What was he to do now? He had no money to buy another horse, and here he was in a lonely lane with no village in sight. London suddenly seemed farther away' than ever. How could he get there now?

All these thoughts raced through his mind as he stood looking at his dead horse; but after a time he decided sadly that the only thing to do was to walk on until he came to some houses where he might get shelter for the night.

So he threw his bag of tools over his shoulder and started trudging wearily down the rough lane. For more than two hours he tramped, feeling more tired and footsore every minute, until at last, to his joy and relief, he saw a few thatched roofs in the distance. Walking as quickly as he could over the rough stones, he reached a small village. Finding the hostelry, he went in to get a room for the night. On entering the traveller's room he looked up wearily—and then suddenly his eyes opened wide. He nearly swooned with joy, for who should be there, talking to the landlord, but the squire of Otley!

Thomas gave a cry of delight which caused the squire to turn round and exclaim:

"Why, bless my soul! If it isn't young Chippendale, the son of the carpenter at Otley. Whatever brings you here in this state? You look half dead."

Thomas went across to him and related his adventures of the last two days and told him that he was trying to get to London.

The squire then said:

"Ah! I seem to remember that as a child you wanted to go to London. So the notion never left your mind, then? But away with you! You are in no fit state to talk now. Go to your bed, and I will see you again in the morning."

So the landlord of the hostelry took Thomas to a bedroom. Being extremely exhausted, he dropped on the bed without waiting to undress and fell immediately into a deep sleep.

He knew no more until he heard the landlord calling to him early the next morning to say that the squire was downstairs waiting to speak to him. Would he hurry and come down?

Thomas jumped off the bed, swilled his face in a bowl of water, and ran downstairs.

"Good morning, Chippendale," said the squire cheerfully as Thomas entered the room. "I trust you feel better after your night's sleep?"

"Truly I do, sir," replied Thomas. "But I am at a loss to know what I am going to do now. I have no horse, so I cannot get to London, nor can I return to Otley."

But the squire answered quickly:

"Have no worry on that score. I have remembered a

promise I made when you were a child. I said that if you became a good carpenter and wanted to work in London I would help you. So go to your room, and fetch your baggage. I am journeying to London, and you can come with me. I have a horse waiting for you."

Thomas could hardly believe his ears. So he would get to London after all! Running joyfully up the stairs, he fetched his bag of tools and was down and outside the hostelry in very quick time.

Four of the squire's serving-men stood holding the bridles of six horses between them. The squire came out of the inn, and they started off. The squire rode in front, while Thomas took his place among the servants following in the rear.

This time the journey was uneventful, and they arrived in London two days later. Thomas was disappointed in the streets when he first rode through them. He had always imagined them to be so different from ordinary streets. They were indeed much grander than any he had seen before, but the houses seemed little better than the squire's at Otley. Nevertheless, he was happy. His lifelong wish had been granted him. He was in London!

When they arrived at the squire's London house the squire gave Thomas a golden sovereign and told him first to get lodgings and then to see him again in a few days' time.

The next week was, for Thomas, the most enjoyable he had ever spent in his life. He roamed the streets admiring the large buildings and watching the fine carriages of the great ladies go by. He spent hours sitting by the River Thames, marvelling at its greatness.

When he again went to see the squire he was told to take his tools to a certain address, where a cabinet-maker would give him work.

When he arrived there he was taken into the workshop

91

by his new master, who had been asked by the squire to give him work. This workshop made Thomas open his eyes wide with astonishment. It was nothing like what he had seen before. Whereas his father's workshop was a tiny room containing a solitary bench, this one was so large that about twenty men were working in it at different benches. And the work they were doing—beautiful cabinets and tables and things such as he had never dreamed it possible to make!

He began to feel nervous and thought to himself:

"I am not clever enough to do this fine work. Would that I had taken notice of my father and stayed at Otley!"

But his master interrupted these thoughts by pointing to a bench and saying:

"That is where you will work. Get your tools ready, and I will give you something to make."

But Thomas need not have been nervous. He soon got into the ways of the workshop and quickly learned how to make this fine furniture. In fact, after a year or two he was thought by his master to be one of his most skilful workmen.

By this time Thomas, realizing how good he had become, had greater ambitions. He wanted now to become his own master and employ other men to do the work for him. So with this in mind he set about saving as much of his wages as he could spare each week. He also went about looking at furniture in showrooms to pick up new ideas and gather fresh knowledge. Whenever he had an opportunity to go into a large house, he would make a careful study of all the kinds of beautiful furniture there and make notes and drawings of it. In this way he learnt much about all the best styles of Chinese, French, English, and Italian furniture then in fashion.

Furthermore, he never missed a chance of making

friends with anyone who might be useful to him later on. If rich people came to the workshop to see how the furniture that was being made for them was progressing, Thomas would take great pains to be pleasant to them and show them how extremely skilful he was.

So time went on, with Thomas continually increasing his skill with his tools, saving more money, and increasing his knowledge, until in the year 1749, after he had been in London for about eight years, he was ready to start a business of his own.

He rented a small workshop in Conduit Court, Long Acre, and began to make cabinets and chairs and other furniture from his own designs. When he had a good stock finished he sent word to the rich people with whom he had made friends and asked them to come to look at his work.

Success came to him quickly. Everybody who went to see his furniture was delighted at its beauty and skilful workmanship. He was starting a fashion in a new style of furniture, and the public liked it. As time went on he received orders to supply furniture to such famous gentlemen as the Duke of Portland, Lord Pembroke, and the Earl of Shaftesbury.

Four years later, in 1753, the business was growing so rapidly that he needed new and bigger workshops so that he could employ more workmen. But he had not yet made enough profits for such a change. He mentioned this to a friend named James Rannie, who said:

"Let us become partners in a new business. I will provide the necessary money to buy the workshops, and I can attend to the office-work while you take charge of the workshops. We will have smart showrooms in a fashionable part of London, and then we shall get all the best people to buy the furniture."

Chippendale quickly agreed to this suggestion, for he

could see that it would help him greatly. His ambition was now to become the most famous cabinet-maker and furniture-designer in the land, and elegant showrooms would go a long way towards showing off his work effectively to the people who mattered.

So the partnership was arranged, and various buildings were inspected to find suitable premises for the new workshops. Eventually Chippendale rented three houses in St Martin's Lane and had them converted into workshops at the back and showrooms at the front.

St Martin's Lane, at that time, was one of the finest streets in London, and many famous people lived there, including Sir Joshua Reynolds, the artist, and David Garrick, the actor.

This new business soon became popular with the rich folk. Chippendale was now a very busy man indeed. His days were spent rushing between his workshop and his showroom. Whenever famous persons came to the showrooms he would conduct them round, taking pains to convince them of the greatness of his work. Then he would go back to the workshop to supervise the work of his many cabinet-makers, carvers, upholsterers, and decorators. He was alert to see that they did their very best work always. He would not allow a shoddy piece of furniture to pass into his showroom.

He also spent much time thinking out new designs for his furniture, and to make sure that the finished article would look as beautiful as he thought it should, he would make a small-scale model of it first. In this way he came to make only the furniture that was worthy of the finest skill of the craftsman.

But for all his success, he was still not satisfied with his lot. Although he now numbered among his customers many famous people, he was ambitious enough to want to be hailed by them as the greatest cabinet-maker living.

94

He thought of a new way in which he might gain his ends. He mentioned it to his partner Rannie:

"We cabinet-makers are only looked upon by the rich as common workmen who are born to attend to their comforts. I am going to make them realize what a great craftsman I am. I am going to publish a book of my designs, so that the rich can buy it and choose from it things they would like made. We shall get more orders that way, and it will help to make the name of Chippendale famous throughout the country."

To Rannie this sounded very boastful, but he replied:

ARMCHAIR: STYLE OF CHIPPENDALE
Victoria and Albert Museum

"The idea of the book seems to be all right, but where are you going to find the money to print it? It will cost a great sum, and you are not sure that the public will buy it."

Chippendale had not thought of this difficulty. He could not, as Rannie said, find enough money for the printing of such an important book. He began to wonder how this obstacle could be surmounted, and after a time another idea struck him.

95

He said to Rannie:

"I have it! I will ask all my wealthy customers to promise to buy a copy of my book. If I get enough promises I can start on the work without any worry about money."

So whenever customers came into the showroom he spoke to them about his book and asked for their assistance. The subscriptions quickly exceeded his hopes. Among his list of subscribers appeared the names of many such famous people as the Marquis of Lothian, Lord Montfort, the Duke of Norfolk, the Duke of Portland, and the Duke of Beaufort.

He also sent out an appeal to all others who might be interested, such as cabinet-makers and carvers who might buy the book to obtain new designs. He soon had enough promises of money to start preparing the book.

He set to work making a large number of accurate drawings of his designs, and employed two engravers to make printing-plates from them. After a few months the book was published in the year 1754 at a cost of £2 8s., or about £6 of present-day money. It is surprising that Chippendale got so many people to pay such a high price for a single book.

The book contained over one hundred and sixty pages of designs, with notes on how to make the furniture from them. The title-page of the book read as follows:

THE GENTLEMAN'S AND CABINET-MAKER'S DIRECTOR

By

THOMAS CHIPPENDALE

Cabinet-maker of St Martin's Lane, London

Being a large collection of the most Elegant and Useful Designs of Household Furniture in the Gothic, Chinese and Modern Taste including a great variety of Book-cases

Library, Writing, Dining and other Tables Buroes Tea-chests Trays Fire-screens Beds Chairs Mirrors Candle-stands Clock-cases and other Ornaments.

The book sold immediately, and in less than twelve months a second edition had to be printed. As Chippendale had hoped, the publication of this book quickly increased his fame. Everybody was now talking about his great ability as a designer and cabinet-maker. Everybody who could afford it wanted his home furnished by Chippendale. So much in demand had the style of his work become that other cabinet-makers tried to copy his designs, but none succeeded well. They had not that superb skill to give the last delicate finish to the carvings, nor could they master the beautiful proportions of Chippendale's furniture.

The wood he now used was mostly mahogany, and he took great care in selecting well-seasoned boards, beauti-fully grained, to give his furniture that solidity and fineness which marked all his work.

In the year 1760 so famous had he become that he was elected a member of the exclusive Royal Society of Arts. This was indeed a great honour for him, because only great artists and sculptors could belong to that society. But had not his beautiful furniture shown him to be a great artist? He had, by his persistence and skill, raised the craft of cabinet-making to the level of the other great arts.

Six years later his partner, James Rannie, died, and for a time Chippendale carried on the work alone. But he soon found that his prosperous business was too much for one man to manage, so he took in another partner, named Thomas Haigh, to do the office-work.

Then, in 1762, a third edition of his *Gentleman's and Cabinet-maker's Director* was published. This time it cost three pounds, because he had added many new designs to suit the changing fashions. He had now turned his attention to designing his cabinets and chairs with beautiful patterns of inlaid coloured woods. This is the furniture we usually associate to-day with the name of Chippendale.

All Chippendale's furniture was very expensive to buy, and only the wealthy could ever think of furnishing their homes with it. Here is one of his bills which shows how much the Duke of Portland paid for two framed mirrors:

His Grace the Duke of Portland Dr.

To Thos. Chippendale

Oct. 28th, 1766

Two very large Oval Glasses with rich carved frames Gilt in burnished Gold with Three Branches for Candles to each and Brass Pans and Nosselles to ditto	£48	- -
Fixing up Ditto at your House	10	-
	£48 10	-

This cost would be about three times as great to-day. But, for all the expensive furniture he sold, Chippendale never became a wealthy man, as many of his customers failed to pay their bills. Here is a letter which shows that he must have been short of money:

To Sir Edward Knatchbull

October 15th, 1770

Sir Edward

I received your letter of the 11th inst and am much obliged to you for sending to me; The £150 will be of great service to me, which is the best way to send it I know not, if any person could give an order payable to me at sight, it would be the readiest way of sending it. If that cannot be done perhaps your banker will pay it if you desire him, you sending the money by the first opportunity. I do not think it safe to send it in Bank Notes as the Mails are so often robbed.

I should be greatly obliged to you if you would do it as fast as possible.

I remain

Your Honoured

Most Obedient and

Most Humble Servant

THO. CHIPPENDALE

In later years Chippendale did a great amount of work for the famous architect Robert Adam. The architect built many great mansions which Chippendale furnished in a manner to suit the design of the buildings.

At the age of sixty-two Chippendale had to take to his bed, and he passed away in November, 1779, having overworked himself for many years in order to realize his ambition of becoming a famous cabinet-maker.

But all the fame and honour his craftsmanship brought to him during his lifetime does not compare with the admiration with which people regard examples of his work to-day, more than one hundred and fifty years after his death. Whenever there is any genuine Chippendale furniture to be sold, wealthy collectors will gather from all parts of the world and pay hundreds of pounds for the privilege of owning a cabinet or book-case made by the great craftsman. It speaks well for Chippendale's skill to know that some of his furniture is as good to-day as when it was made.

VI

JOHN SMEATON

Mathematical-instrument Maker

Two hundred years ago Leeds, now one of the most important cities in Yorkshire, was nothing more than a

tiny market town of a few straggling streets surrounded by fields and woodlands. Its present great industry, the weaving and manufacture of woollen cloths, was then so small that the cloth-market was held in the open air, the bales of cloth for sale being displayed on the parapets of the river bridge.

Machinery had not at this time been invented, and each weaver laboriously wove his lengths of cloth on his simple hand-loom in his cottage. Each week he would take his cloths to the bridge, lay them out on the parapet, and wait to bargain for them with anybody who might want to make a suit or a dress and had come along to the market to buy some suitable cloth.

Transport was also very primitive and slow. Carts and wagons were seldom used, because the badly made roads would soon smash up their wheels; instead, pack-horses were the chief means of carrying food, coal, and cloths from one town to another. The horses had large panniers, or baskets, strapped to their sides, and these were filled with wares of various descriptions.

One of the chief townsmen of Leeds at this time was a solicitor named Smeaton. He lived in a large house, called Austhorpe Lodge, situated on the outskirts of the town. The house was gloriously situated in a surrounding of green fields and beautiful woodlands.

Mr Smeaton was a prosperous man and lived in the style of a gentleman. He had an office in the main street of Leeds, to which most of the townsmen brought their problems for him to deal with.

The happiest day in the lives of both Mr Smeaton and his wife came on the eighth of June in the year 1724, when a son, whom they named John, was born to them. They had for years longed for a son, and now that their wish had been granted they were overjoyed.

Mr Smeaton said to his wife, "Now that we have a son he will be able to follow in my footsteps and carry on my work when I am getting old. I will take him into my office and teach him all I know, and one day he may become a great lawyer."

John grew up into a strong, healthy boy under the loving care of his fond parents. Much of his time was spent at play in the woods and fields round his home. He loved to help the farmer take the cows back to the sheds for milking-time and to listen to the strange tales the shepherd told him as he tended his sheep on the grassy slopes.

There were few schools in the country when John was young, so his mother gave him his lessons at home in the mornings. A child was indeed lucky in those days if he were able to learn to read and write, because very few had the opportunity. Only those parents who were wealthy and had been educated themselves or could afford to pay expensive fees to private tutors could ever hope to give their children any schooling.

John was a bright boy and learned to read and write at a very early age. His parents were delighted with his progress. They wanted him to become a good scholar, for they were both anxious that he should become, like his father, a solicitor, and for that work one had to be able to read and write well.

John was not very keen on his lessons, though. He soon realized that it was much more fun playing with the few tools his father kept in the wash-house at the bottom of the garden. When he was very young he began to use the tools to build up little toys and models which he could play with. He was always contriving something which he thought might work. Hours upon end he would spend nailing together pieces of wood, making models of houses, ships, wagons, and windmills. He never seemed to be greatly interested in anything except in making these working models.

He never went to play in the streets with other boys, and they all thought him to be a queer kind of lad. Whenever he went out they would call after him, "There goes fooley Smeaton, who is afraid to play with us." It was not that John was afraid, though; it was just that he found far greater enjoyment in playing with his father's tools.

Whenever there were carpenters or builders working in the district near his home he would go and stand for hours watching, with great fascination, the way in which they skilfully handled their tools. He would pester them with questions such as:

"What is that tool called? What do you use it for? How are you going to fit those pieces of wood together?"

The carpenters would answer him until they were tired of his numerous questions and then tell him to run off home and stop being a nuisance. But often John would not move. He was anxious to learn all he could about using tools properly.

Once he went to watch some workmen who had come to build a pump in the street. He soon learned from them how the pump worked and took great care to notice how the parts were fitted together.

When the workmen had finished their work and were packing up their tools, John said to one of them:

"Can you give me a piece of that lead-piping you have left, please?"

"What on earth do you want that for?" inquired the workman. "It is of no use for anything except for making pumps and such-like things."

"That is just what I want it for. To make a pump with!" answered John without hesitation.

At this statement the workman burst out laughing and said, "What? A youngster like you talking about making a pump! Why, that is a man's job, and far too hard for a little boy to do. But you might as well have this odd piece of piping to play with. It will save me the trouble of carrying it away."

Delightedly John grabbed the piece of piping as the workman threw it towards him and ran off home to start building his pump. The workman's words had not disheartened him. He had learnt from him how a pump was made, and he could use tools; so why should he not be able to make one himself? Anyway, he resolved to have a good try.

He spent every spare minute he had for the next four days in hammering and chiselling in the wash-house, building his model pump. As soon as it was finished he was eager to see if it would act and pump up water like the one the workmen had built.

So he took it into the garden with the intention of going into the house and filling the kitchen sink with water and trying it there; but before he reached the house his eyes fell upon the fishpond in the middle of the lawn. This gave him an idea.

"Just the very place!" he thought. "The pond holds a good depth of water, so I shall be able to give it a good testing."

Going across to the pond, he placed the suction-pipe of his model into the water and began to work the pumping-handle up and down.

To his delight, the surface of the pond-water began to gurgle, and after a moment or two of vigorous pumping, gushes of water began to spurt on to the grass at every pull of the handle. His model was working! The workman had been wrong in his estimation of the skill of this young boy.

So interested was John in his new toy that he kept on working the handle and watching the water spurt out and soak through the surface of the lawn, but he failed to notice what was happening in the fishpond. He had drained it practically dry! The poor goldfish were floundering in the bottom, vainly struggling for their lives.

Not until the pump had given a last gurgle and stopped drawing water did he look up and notice, to his profound astonishment and horror, what he had done. By this time the fish were beyond help. He had seen their plight too late.

He began to wonder what he should do, but before he had time to think of anything his father came out of the house to look for him. Glancing at the pond, he opened his eyes wide with astonishment at what he saw and exclaimed sharply:

"My goodness, John! Whatever have you been doing?"

"I—I am s-sorry, Father," stammered John nervously, "but I made a pump and tried it in the pond, and I was so interested in seeing it work that I did not notice what was happening to the pond until it was empty."

"Well, you should notice! Now you have killed all my goldfish," stormed his father angrily. "You are always up to some mischief with your silly tools. If you cannot use them sensibly I will forbid you to have them."

After this unlucky incident John was more careful with his experiments, but he continued to find great happiness in making things which would work.

On his tenth birthday his father bought him a good set of tools and had a real carpenter's bench fixed up in the wash-house for him. He could see that John was becoming very clever with tools, and he thought it right to encourage him in his hobby.

By this time John was attending a private school in Leeds and showed great cleverness at arithmetic, geometry, and drawing. He was now able to make neat and accurate drawings of the models he made.

By the age of fifteen he had become so skilful at working with both wood and metal that he was able to make a real lathe machine for his own use. With it he made many little round jewel-boxes, chessmen of bone and ivory, and other small articles, which he gave to his friends.

Then on his sixteenth birthday his father said to him:

"It is now time for you to leave school, John, and start to work and learn your profession of a lawyer. I will arrange for you to come with me to the office each day. You must make up your mind to work and study hard, and then in time you will be able to take charge of the office for me."

But John was not at all anxious to do as his father wished. He would much rather have worked for a craftsman who would teach him more about using his tools than work in a stuffy office. But he knew that it was his parents' wish that he should become a lawyer, so he decided to be a dutiful son and say nothing about his own desires.

So he started to work in his father's office. He quickly found, though, that he hated the work of poring all day and every day over great ledgers, adding up figures and writing out legal documents. It held no interest for him at all. He was always glad when tea-time came, so that he could get home to his little work-bench in the wash-house. He was continually making mistakes at the office which made his father cross, but he just could not settle his mind to his work. Instead he would always be thinking about what he could make next with his tools.

One day, after his father had been reprimanding him for a serious mistake he had made, John told him his trouble. He said:

"Father, I shall never become a good lawyer. I must confess to you that I do not like the work, and I cannot set myself to learn it as you would wish. Much rather would I work for a craftsman so that I could use my hands to make things. Then I would be happy."

His father replied sympathetically:

"For a long time now I have noticed that you have shown no interest at your desk, John, and much as I regret it, I quite understand your desires; much as I have wanted to make you become a lawyer, I can now see that it is useless for me to try. Therefore I will let you have your wish. I will inquire and find a good craftsman who will employ you and teach you to do his work."

JOHN SMEATON

John thanked his father profusely for his great generosity. He knew how much it hurt him to give him his wish. But he was happy for himself. He was now going to do the work he loved, and the prospects for his future seemed to him extremely bright.

True to his word, Mr Smeaton told John, less than a week later, that he had arranged with a clever mathematical-instrument maker in London to teach him his craft and that he was to start his new work as soon as possible.

John was in a state of great excitement all the way to London. The journey by stage-coach seemed endless, so anxious was he to get there. After four days' travelling he arrived in London, sought out his new master, and started work.

The master soon found that John was very skilful with tools of all descriptions and gave him many different kinds of delicate instruments to repair. For the first few months of John's stay in London Mr Smeaton had to send him money each week to pay for his food and lodgings, but after that John's master was so pleased with the progress of his new pupil that he raised his wages sufficiently for him to keep himself.

John continued to work for his master until the year 1750, when, at the age of twenty-six, he started a business of his own as an instrument-maker.

It was not long before his cleverness at repairing instruments became known, and he was given plenty of work to do. He also spent much time in experimenting with and improving the different kinds of instruments then in use. He constructed a mariner's compass which was a great improvement over any which had been made before. He also invented a new instrument for measuring the direction in which a ship was sailing on the sea. His clever work with scientific and mathematical instruments soon brought his name to the notice of the famous group of great scientists known as the Royal Society. Before large audiences of famous scientists he was often asked to give lectures on his work of improving instruments. In this way he soon became quite well known for his work as a craftsman and inventor.

But although his business prospered and he had little need to bother about money matters, he still worked extremely hard to improve his knowledge. He learnt to read French so that he would be able to read the scientific books written in that language.

He had also begun to take a great interest in such engineering-work as the building of bridges, harbours, and canals. Although he had no intention of giving up his work as an instrument-maker, this new subject of engineering fascinated him and proved to be an absorbing hobby. In 1754 he made a special journey to Holland to inspect and study the methods of the great Dutch engineers who had covered their land with dykes and canals.

His knowledge of the subject grew so great that often engineers would ask his advice as to how they should build their bridges and canals. He would then help them to design these without charge.

Then, although he was as surprised as anyone when it happened, he soon had an opportunity to put his knowledge of engineering to the test.

It happened in this way. Many years previously, numerous ships were continually being wrecked each winter on the dangerous rocks at Eddystone, fourteen miles out to sea from Plymouth. There was a great outcry among the people for something to be done to protect the ships and sailors from these great dangers. A lighthouse was needed on the rock to guide the ships safely at night, but nobody dared attempt the difficult and dangerous job of building one.

Eventually an enterprising business man named Winstanley decided to try to build one and charge each ship as it passed by a sum of money for the safe guidance the lighthouse afforded it.

Everybody thought that he must be mad to attempt such a dangerous task. "It is impossible to build anything on such a dangerous rock as the Eddystone," they said. But Winstanley took little notice of anybody and proceeded to build his lighthouse. He found the work far more difficult and dangerous than he had expected, but he persevered and had it finished in the year 1700—four years after he had started. The lighthouse was an odd kind of affair built entirely of wood, with a balcony at the top for displaying the light to guide the ships. People laughed when they saw this lighthouse and said that it

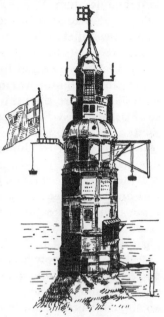

THE FIRST EDDYSTONE LIGHTHOUSE

would not stand up to the violent winter storms. Winstanley was so sure that it would that he went to live in it and wished that the greatest storm ever known would come to test it. Unfortunately, the storm did come on a winter's night three years later, and the lighthouse was blown away, with Winstanley in it.

The next winter a richly laden ship was wrecked on the Eddystone rock, and all aboard perished. This raised an outcry from sailors everywhere for a new lighthouse.

For a long time nobody would attempt to build one,

but at last another business man, named John Rudyerd, came along in 1706 and said he would take charge of building a new one. He designed his lighthouse in a much better style than Winstanley had done, and made the sides cone-shaped to avoid corners and flat sides which might be buffeted by the violent winds. His lighthouse took three years to build, and towards the end of the year 1709 the lantern was lit for the first time.

But this lighthouse was mainly built of timber. Although it stood for more than fifty years, battling with the great storms which swept across the English Channel each winter, it was burnt down in 1755, when the candles which were used to illuminate the lantern set fire to the wooden walls.

By this time the ships on the sea were many, and so there was an urgent need for another lighthouse on the Eddystone rock to take the place of Rudyerd's ill-fated one. During the next winter there were a great many wrecks with much loss of life.

A Mr Weston now became the owner of the Eddystone, and he decided to find somebody who was capable of erecting a new and stronger lighthouse on the dreaded rock. But all the engineers he asked refused to have anything to do with it; they said that the work was too dangerous for any man to attempt.

In despair Mr Weston went to the President of the Royal Society to see if he could recommend a scientist or engineer who would take charge of the building-work. He said to the President:

"There is a great need for a new lighthouse on the Eddystone. The ship's captains are finding great difficulty in steering their way up the Channel at night, now that Rudyerd's light has gone. I want to find a man who has the ability and the courage to go out to that dangerous rock and on it erect a new lighthouse which will stand firm and strong against the most violent storms and seas. I have come to you because you are the most likely person to know of somebody who will undertake this work. Can you give me the name of anyone?"

Without hesitation the President replied:

"I know the very man you are looking for. His name is John Smeaton, and although he works as a mathematical-instrument maker, he also has great ability and a profound knowledge of engineering-science. If he will consent to build your lighthouse you need have no fear as to its strength and safety, I assure you, for Smeaton will not undertake to do the work unless he is absolutely certain that he can carry it out."

Mr Weston thanked him for his help and went off to the house of John Smeaton. He explained his business to him and asked John if he thought he could do the work. John thought for some time before answering, but eventually said:

"I do not feel that I can spare the time to build this lighthouse, Mr Weston, as I am so busy with my other work. But somebody must do it, for the sake of the lives of the many sailors who need it in winter; so, if you wish, I will consider the matter and give you my answer in a few days."

Mr Weston agreed to this and left John to think about this new kind of problem. John could see that a colossal task lay before him if he undertook to do the work, but the idea of overcoming such an obstacle intrigued him. The more he thought about it, the more he wanted to tell Mr Weston that he had decided to do it. But he had to make sure that he was capable of it first.

He began to wonder how he would design the light-house. He obtained plans of both Winstanley's and Rudyerd's buildings and studied them carefully. He made a list of all the defects he could find in them and quickly came to the conclusion that wood was a useless material for a lighthouse. He thought that one built of stone would be much better and stronger. His friends disagreed with this, saying that nothing but a wooden structure would stand for long on that dangerous rock. If such a slender, lofty building was constructed of stone the top of it would be too heavy and would be blown off in the first gale, they said.

John also realized that the shape of the lighthouse must be such that it was strong enough to make the rough sea give way to it. After studying various shapes he finally decided that the cone shape used by Rudyerd was far stronger than any other. He was becoming extremely interested in this new work, and he badly wanted to build the lighthouse. When Smeaton was given a problem to do, he rarely gave it up until he had solved it.

He spent many hours with blocks of wood as models of the stones he would use for the walls, cutting them about and fitting them together to discover the best joints to use to bind each stone firmly to the next. He experimented with various kinds of cement to find the best one to use in the foundations. For weeks he continued experimenting with many kinds of materials, and at last he set about designing the shape of his lighthouse.

Mr Weston visited him periodically to see how he was progressing, but John kept putting him off a little longer each time. He was not prepared to rush to do the job until he was sure that he was fully prepared. So, although Weston was becoming very impatient, he could do nothing but wait for John to say that he was ready to start building.

In 1756 John made a journey to Plymouth to survey and measure up the Eddystone rock, on which the lighthouse was to be built. On his first trip out to the rock the sea was too rough to allow him to land, and he had to return to Plymouth to await a calmer day. But the weather did not seem to change, and he made several more trips, only to return as he did the first time without landing on the rock. He began to wonder how he could ever manage to build a lighthouse there if he were not even able to land. But he persevered in his daily trips, and at last was able to land for the purpose of measuring up and closely examining the Eddystone.

He next made trips to all the stone quarries near Plymouth to select a suitable stone for building the walls of the lighthouse. He finally decided to use Portland stone encased in blocks of granite, as that seemed to be harder and more durable than any other.

Then he returned to London and went to see Mr Weston.

He said to him:

"At last I have finished considering your proposal, and now I am prepared to build your lighthouse. It will be constructed of stone and will be so strong that it will stand firm against any storm or tempest, I feel sure. I have prepared my designs and am ready to start building it as soon as you give me your permission."

"That is good news," replied Weston. "I was beginning to think that I should never find anybody with enough courage and skill to attempt this work. But before you start I should like to know how you propose to build it."

John answered, "That I can best explain to you by building a model of the building exactly as I propose to build the real one. If you will be patient for a few more days I shall bring you back a model which will show you everything you want to know. Then you can decide for yourself if you think it worth going on with."

So Smeaton went back to his workshop and built his model. He took great pains to build it in every way just as he proposed to erect the real one. Each stone of the walls was made from a tiny block of wood exactly shaped and fitted to the next. The lantern and lighthouse-keeper's rooms were all included in miniature.

When Weston saw it he was delighted and gave Smeaton permission to start building immediately.

John thereupon went down to Plymouth and engaged workmen who were strong and skilful. He ordered materials such as stone, wood, and cement, and bought vessels to take the men and materials out to the rock. He appointed a clever shipwright, named Mr Jessop, to take charge of the workmen, and everything was ready to start on August 3, 1756.

A store-ship was taken out to sea and anchored near the rock. On this were kept food and water for the workmen, for they were to sleep on it at nights in order to save the time sailing backward and forward to the rock each day.

Work was begun on laying the foundations of the building, but Smeaton soon found many difficulties in his way. The men could only work for six hours each day, while the tide was low, for at all other times the sea washed over the rock and would have drowned them. Often they worked at night with the aid of torches, so that they should miss no opportunity of getting on before the bad weather set in. Sometimes such storms would rage that it was impossible to go on the rock for days on end.

One night such a violent storm arose that the store-ship broke its anchor and began to drift towards the dreaded Bay of Biscay. Smeaton and his men did everything possible to combat the storm, but they were helpless. It seemed as though the end had come. Smeaton's chief worry was that he would not live to finish the lighthouse. For four days and nights the ship was buffeted and battered in the wind; then, as suddenly as it had begun, the storm abated, and they were able to sail back to Plymouth safe and sound.

The winter was so rough and stormy that no attempt was made to reach the rock; instead, the men filled in the time by working at Plymouth, preparing and cutting the stones ready for building the walls when next they could get to work on the rock.

Work started again in the spring. The foundations were soon laid, and the first block of stone was placed in its position by Smeaton on Sunday, June 12, 1757.

When the walls had been built above the level to which the sea rose, the men were able to work more quickly and for longer hours. But again Smeaton and his men had to give up work and sail back to Plymouth at the first signs of winter.

The cry from sailors for a guiding-light grew more persistent during this winter. They thought that Smeaton was very slow in his work and urged him to hurry with it. They did not realize the difficulties and dangers his men had to face if they attempted to land on the rock during the winter. To satisfy the sailors for the time being, Smeaton moored a temporary lightship off the rock; but it broke away in a storm and was smashed to pieces on the rocks.

Each morning during this winter Smeaton would go to the harbour with his telescope to look at the rock. He was afraid each morning that he would find the foundations of his lighthouse to have been washed away during the night.

As they proceeded to sail out for the first time during the next spring Smeaton with his mind full of doubt, said to Jessop:

"I hope everything will be all right on the rock. I am so afraid that when we get there we shall find that all our work has been done in vain. I wonder if the cement has held out against the storms? Perhaps the foundations have weakened. There is no telling what might have happened in six months on that perilous rock."

But his doubts were soon relieved. On reaching the

SMEATON'S EDDYSTONE LIGHTHOUSE

rock he made a quick examination of everything and found, to his joy, that the cement had set as hard as the stones themselves, and not a stone had moved from its place.

He now felt more confident that his lighthouse would defy the most violent gales, although engineers everywhere still thought he was wasting his time and continued to say that no stone building could ever stand for long on the Eddystone rock.

Work proceeded rapidly through the summer, and by August 12, 1759, the cone-shaped wall towered into the sky for a height of seventy feet. It looked so slender and tall from the Sound at Plymouth that every one who saw it felt certain that the first storm would blow it over.

But Smeaton went on with his work. The balcony and lantern were fixed, Smeaton himself driving in the last screws. The light was lit for the first time on the sixteenth of October of the same year.

Imagine Smeaton's anxiety now that the next winter was drawing near! Was his building as strong as he thought, or would he see three years' work wasted by its being shattered in the first gale? Seventy feet of towering stone waiting to face all weathers!

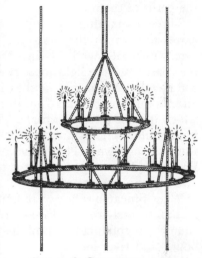

SMEATON'S CHANDELIER, 1759

So anxious was he that he resolved to live in the lighthouse for the first winter to watch the effects of the storms and gales upon it.

The winter passed. Tempestuous seas and howling winds frequently beat against the stonework, but the lighthouse continued to shine its warning light to the passing ships at night.

Smeaton was satisfied. He had performed a masterpiece of engineering which everybody had thought impossible. His name was on everybody's lips. Congratulations poured in upon him from sailors, engineers, and great scientists. They were all high in their praises for his great feat of skill. His lighthouse had become the means of saving thousands of lives each winter from the dangers of the Eddystone rock. Smeaton's great enterprise gave the lead to others to build lighthouses all round the coast of the British Isles, so as to make ships safe from the perils of the rocks.

Three years after the lighthouse had shown its light across the sea for the first time, the most terrible storm ever witnessed raged for days, ruining everything along the coast. But the lighthouse stood the test. It remained completely undamaged, and so it stood for one hundred and twenty-three years—until 1882, when the rock on which it stood became unsafe. Then Sir James Douglass built another one on another rock near by, and Smeaton's was taken down. The upper sections were rebuilt on Plymouth Hoe as a monument to the great courage and skill of John Smeaton.

When Smeaton returned to London after his great work, he immediately received many requests from all over the country to conduct the building of bridges, canals, harbours, and river-locks.

He had so many offers of engineering-work that he gave up his business as a mathematical-instrument maker to carry them out. Many of the bridges now standing in Great Britain, especially in Scotland, were designed and erected by Smeaton.

But for all the prosperity and fame which had now come his way, he never gave up his work with his tools, and he continued to invent new instruments and machines in his spare time. Among other things he made an improved pumping-engine and a blowing-apparatus for smelting iron.

He also tried to develop the steam-engine, which was quite a recent invention, and erected a fairly good one at his house at Leeds. But he was not particularly successful with this, because just when he had finished it, James Watt invented a much better one. Smeaton, with the spirit of a true craftsman, then wrote to Watt and congratulated him on his success, scrapping his own engine.

John Smeaton died at the age of sixty-eight on the twenty-eighth of October, 1792, happy in the knowledge that he had been the means of saving the lives of many of our fearless sailors, who are always risking the fury of storm and tempest to bring food to our homes from overseas.

VII
JOSIAH WEDGWOOD
Potter

ONE often reads in the newspaper that workmen engaged on digging have unearthed some pieces of Roman

JOSIAH WEDGWOOD
National Portrait Gallery

pottery. Perhaps a vase or a fragment of one, sometimes an urn or dish, and occasionally quite a large collection of assorted articles are found together within a small area. It is interesting to realize that these pieces of pottery had, until disturbed by the picks and spades of the workmen, remained buried for more than two thousand years—from the time when the Romans invaded and settled in England.

These 'finds' are very useful to our historians, for they help them to piece together the story of how the people of those days lived and worked. Sometimes signs are found on the surface of the pottery which, when deciphered, tell us about the habits and customs of these people.

JOSIAH WEDGWOOD

Even the Romans were not the first people who learned how to fashion beautiful and useful articles in clay. The earlier Egyptian races and many primitive races before them had already discovered that baked clay could be put to many uses. In fact, pottery-making is one of the oldest crafts known to man.

Nevertheless, until about two hundred years ago the British people were not very clever in fashioning articles from clay. A little of the art was learnt from the Roman settlers, but after these returned to their own country the skill of the Britons declined. So we find that the people living in the early eighteenth century were using cups, plates, and dishes made of a common rough red pottery, the surface of which was similar to that of a brick—not a very suitable material from which to make a drinking-cup.

At this time the potters carried on their work in their own cottages, digging up the clay from the neighbouring fields and fashioning their utensils in the kitchen.

Let us try to imagine what one of these potter's kitchens was like. A potter's wheel, a circular horizontal board mounted on a stand, which would revolve at a good speed when the potter worked the treadle attached, would be under the window of the kitchen. Near by, a table would be seen loaded with moist balls of grey clay side by side with a number of articles such as plates, dishes, and jars still in the clayey state. In a corner would be found a small oven, in which the shaped clay was baked, or 'fired.' The potter would spend his days at the wheel, throwing balls of moist clay on to the centre of the revolving board and quickly and deftly shaping each ball in turn into a bowl or dish. All the work was done with the fingers, and a skilful potter could 'throw,' as the shaping of the clay is called, a pot in a very short time. The pots were placed in the oven in batches to be 'fired' and made ready for sale.

The selling of the potter's work was no easy task in those days, because the earthenware articles had to be carted in crates slung over the backs of pack-horses and hawked round the cottages in near-by villages. The crates-man had no enviable job. He would load up his horse at the potter's cottage and set off along the muddy, narrow country lanes to the villages round. How difficult it must have been for him to prevent the horse from slipping in pot-holes in the badly made lanes and to save smashing his wares! He could not even let his horse jog along, for fear of knocking the pottery together in the crates and so causing breakages.

The potters lived mostly in the villages and towns of Staffordshire, the county which is still the centre of our pottery-industry. Our story now takes us to one of these villages, called Burslem, which has since become a large industrial town full of great modern pottery-factories. It was then a scattered village of thatched cottages on the top of a hill. On entering the village, a traveller would have had no difficulty in finding out what the local industry was. He would not need to ask, for the sign of all the fields round, disfigured by the rough patches and pits made by the potters in digging up the clay, would be sufficient to tell him.

One family of potters living in Burslem at this time went by the name of Wedgwood. The Wedgwoods had gained a good name in the district as excellent workmen, and people used to say, "Nobody round here can make a pot like Wedgwood. The shape is always good, the surface is smooth, and it never wobbles when set down." Naturally the Wedgwoods sold more articles than any of the other potters and became one of the best-known makers in the district.

At about this time, in the year 1730 to be exact, Josiah Wedgwood, the hero of our story, was born into this family. At a very early age he began to help with digging and preparing the clay for his father to 'throw,' and soon became interested in his family's craft of pottery-making. This was really only natural, seeing that he was living in and round the workroom.

By the time that he was ten years old he was often to be found in the family's workroom, practising the craft of pottery with his brother. He would proudly show each piece of pottery he had made to his father and ask, "What do you·think of this, Father? Do you think I shall ever become a clever potter like you? Is this one an improvement on the jug I showed you last week?"

His father would take Josiah's work in his hands, twist and turn it about to detect the faults, and, after a pause, answer, "Yes, it shows an improvement, Josiah, but there are still faults in it. Look here," he would say, pointing to the curved side of the article. "Do you not think this curve is ugly? A little more skill when 'throwing' will put that right. Then the base is too small. This pot could be easily knocked over and broken. You must always remember to make your work suitable for use. And remember, too, that, however well you do your work, there are others who could do it better. So you must never be satisfied. Always strive to do the next job better than the previous one."

These criticisms from his father gave Josiah the desire to become the greatest potter ever known. In his boyish dreams he could see himself when he grew up being praised by peoples from all parts of the world. Every time he made an article on his father's wheel he strove to make it better than his last.

Then misfortune befell him when he was eleven years old. A plague of smallpox was raging over Staffordshire, and one evening Josiah felt ill. His mother noticed that spots were coming out on his face, and she said, "Father, get the doctor along. I think Josiah has caught the plague."

"Do not get worried, my dear," replied Mr Wedgwood, trying to banish her fears. "It may only be some common rash."

But sure enough, when the doctor arrived Josiah was found to be suffering from the dreaded disease. Luckily, after many weeks of anxiety for his family, Josiah recovered, but the disease had left its mark on him. His right knee became stiff and paralysed. This was a great catastrophe, as he could not now treadle the potter's wheel at which he so yearned to become a great craftsman.

For three years he did no more to his beloved craft. Then, at the age of fourteen, as his leg began to show signs of getting better, his father made him an apprentice to learn the art of 'throwing.' But at sixteen the illness returned, and he had to be found lighter jobs about the workshop.

It gave Josiah great pain and sadness to have to give up his work, which he enjoyed so much, so, at the age of nineteen, he decided to try again. He approached his brother. "Why not start a business together?" he suggested. "We could do well as master potters. We know the work and each other's skill. Father will lend us the money to buy our tools with."

"You would be of no use as a partner," replied the brother rudely. "Why, you cannot even use a 'wheel,' with your leg as it is. I want a partner who can share the work as well as the profits. No, I would not consider it for a moment."

Naturally to be snubbed like this by one's own brother was a great blow to Josiah's pride, and he resolved there and then to find another partner and set up a business which would become known far and wide.

Eventually he met another potter, named Thomas

Whieldon, who agreed to become his partner. They worked hard together and made a very successful business of it. During this partnership Wedgwood began to study the various kinds of clay, experimenting with different mixtures, painting and coating the pots with chemicals to see what effect the baking would have on them. He was trying to prepare a kind of pottery which would be better than that of any other potter. Eventually he discovered a mixture of clay and chemicals which, when baked, appeared coated with a beautiful blue glaze. He showed it to his partner, Whieldon, and they both agreed to start making all their ware with this mixture. It met with a ready sale. The people in the neighbourhood had never seen such beautiful jugs, basins, and pitchers before, and they were anxious to buy them.

This partnership with Whieldon lasted for six years, and then, in the year 1759, Wedgwood decided to work alone. He took over a small house in Burslem, known as "Ivy House," and employed a cousin as potter, as he was not capable of spending long days at the wheel himself. The business soon grew, until he had to employ a number of workmen.

Often he would go to one of the wheels in the workshop and then surprise his workmen with his remarkable skill by 'throwing' a beautiful vase in quicker time than they could do it.

Wedgwood always insisted on the very best work from his workmen, and he sometimes said to them, "The articles you make here must be as good to use as they are to look at. What is the use of making a beautiful jug if it won't pour? Far better that it should be ugly and pour well. But it is best that it should both pour well and be beautiful."

Inspired by their master's words, these workmen used to make the best pottery in Staffordshire, and everybody began to hear of Wedgwood pottery. People used to say of this pottery, "The lids fitted, the spouts poured, and the handles held." Others would remark, "Dozens of plates can be piled up without breaking, so exactly do they correspond in size and shape." What better advertisements could Wedgwood want? Even his workmen used

BLACK BASALTIC WARE TEA-POT
Victoria and Albert Museum

to make fun of the saying, "That won't do for Josiah Wedgwood," when one of them had made a mistake. But how true it was! Wedgwood would not let a thing leave his workshop unless it had been made perfectly.

As the business grew, Wedgwood kept introducing new methods and ideas into the workshop. New kinds of kilns for 'firing' the pots and new time-saving methods were tried out, so that the work might proceed more effectively and the prices of his wares be reduced. All the time he was experimenting with different clays and chemicals. He was always prepared to spend large sums of money to obtain samples of new clays from different parts of the world. Added to all this work, he was a great reader, and was interested in many subjects, such as astronomy, engineering, and art. He spent much of his spare money on expensive books.

As his pottery-works grew he found it necessary to obtain most of his clay from the china-clay pits in Cornwall. This had to be shipped to Liverpool and carted from there to Burslem by road, making the cost of the clay much greater. Consequently he saw the need for some form of transport which would carry the clay to the potteries from Liverpool quickly and cheaply. A canal, he thought, was the most suitable method. But canals cost much money to build. He did not know how it could be done. Nevertheless, he had heard that the great Bridgewater Canal, running from Manchester to Liverpool, had just been completed by a famous engineer named James Brindley, so he made a journey to Liverpool to see him.

After Wedgwood had explained his scheme to Brindley he asked him what he thought of it.

Brindley thought for a while and said, "A canal such as you need would be a great asset to the potters of Staffordshire, not only for the purpose of carrying clay from Liverpool, but also for taking pottery-ware to the great towns of the north. It would help your trade to expand. But it would be a very expensive job to cut such a great canal as you propose. Nevertheless, come and see me again, and I will design a suitable canal and work out its approximate cost in the meantime."

When Wedgwood got back to Burslem he called together a meeting of the local potters and explained the idea to them. He thought they would all subscribe towards the cost.

"What a chance it will be for us," he said. "Now we have to wait weeks for our clay, but with a canal it would mean days. And the barges could go back laden with our finished pottery. Look at what that would mean to our trade!"

He made a long speech, but he did not impress them much with the idea. "What is the use of getting more trade if we have got to spend hundreds of thousands of pounds first to get it?" asked one. "We shall all be ruined before the canal is finished."

He came away from the meeting disappointed at his failure, but determined to carry on with the scheme. As soon as he arrived home he wrote a number of letters to his friends to try to persuade them to join him in subscribing the money necessary to commence building. To his great joy most of his friends agreed to take large shares in the scheme, and so he found himself with enough money to start the work. Enthusiastically he wrote to Brindley telling him of his success and asking him to start work as soon as possible.

July 26, 1766, the day on which the canal was started, was made a gala day in Burslem. Everybody took a holiday and joined together in festivities in celebration of the great event in their lives. A sheep was roasted on the spot where the canal was started, as a symbol of new prosperity for the local potteries.

A great crowd gathered to watch Wedgwood dig the first barrow-load of earth for the canal, while Brindley, the engineer-in-charge, wheeled it away. The rejoicings were carried on until a late hour that night.

Brindley made an excellent job of the canal, and it is still in use to this day, being now known as the Grand Trunk Canal.

In a very few months after the first barges had gone away from Burslem, loaded with pottery, to find new markets, Wedgwood's business began to increase very rapidly.

Burslem was growing fast, new potteries were springing

up, and orders were being received from all parts of England. Wedgwood's china was becoming fashionable in the smart homes in London. The well-to-do-people were discussing its merits wherever they went, and Wedgwood's fame was spreading rapidly. Eminent personages were beginning to collect these delicately shaped Wedgwood vases to adorn the rooms of their mansions. The news of this smart pottery had spread even to America, and a new export-trade was started.

This business with American buyers often took Wedgwood to Liverpool to arrange the transport across the sea. On one of his first visits there in this connexion he met a city merchant by the name of Bentley, who was later to play a great part in Wedgwood's life. Wedgwood found Bentley to be a very charming companion, of wide education and experience. Bentley quickly felt a great liking for this potter, who, although now well on the pathway to fame and fortune, still retained his unaffected friendliness and modesty. The two men became great friends, and both looked forward with pleasure to each time that they could meet and discuss the latest news about books, art, astronomy, and engineering.

But Wedgwood was beginning to find that he was becoming overwhelmed with work. These journeys to Liverpool were not allowing him sufficient time to control his works and make his experiments with clays. His little pottery at "Ivy House" was fast becoming too small for the masses of orders that were continually flowing in. Something had to be done about it quickly. He decided that the first need was for some one to join him as a partner in the business. Who would be suitable? His thought immediately went to his greatest friend, Bentley.

"If only I could persuade him to join me! But will he relinquish his own merchant's business and risk starting in a work about which he knows nothing? I am doubtful, but I will put the proposition before him when I am next in his company." As Wedgwood feared, Bentley was dubious about the suggestion that was put before him.

"I may be useless in a business which is strange to me. If I sell my business and then find that I am of no use to you, I shall be sorry I ever thought of it. Furthermore, it will mean that I exile myself from my friends in Liverpool, and I am rather old to start life anew."

For a long time the discussion went on, and eventually Wedgwood persuaded him to become a partner.

The next step in the progress of the business was to find larger premises to cope with the increasing amount of work. A site for a factory was chosen on the bank of the new canal, so that the barges could be unloaded of clay and loaded again with pottery at little cost. He had all the new ideas of which he had heard incorporated in the design to make the work run more smoothly. Newly invented kilns were installed in special rooms; large rooms were built for each separate process of pottery-manufacture. There were rooms for the clay-mixers, the 'throwers,' the artists who painted designs on the surface of the china, and the modellers.

On the day the new Etruria Works, as Wedgwood called his factory, was opened, the master potter himself took the clay in his hands, seated himself at the 'thrower's' bench, and 'threw' the first vase into shape. Bentley took charge of the office and kept the accounts in order, so that Wedgwood might have more time to supervise the workmen and experiment with new clay mixtures.

It was at this time becoming fashionable to buy vases and other china ornaments which had figure-designs on the surface similar to those executed by the ancient Greeks. Wedgwood was continually trying to obtain accurate copies of these Greek vases. He was not satisfied with the colours and clays which were being used in the manufacture of these copies. He went to great pains to obtain new clays and colour-powders, taking careful note of the different proportions in which he mixed them. In this way he dis-covered recipes for many new kinds of earthenware.

The business was now growing so rapidly that the partners saw the need for an elegant showroom in Lon-don, where the new kinds of pottery might be displayed. So, with many mis-givings and much sadness on the part of Wedgwood at the thought of los-ing his beloved companion, it was decided that Bent-ley should live in London and take charge of the busi-ness there. Very soon after the show-room was opened

JASPER WARE VASE
Victoria and Albert Museum
By permission of H.M. Stationery Office

it became fashionable for the rich to go there to view the pottery from Etruria Works. Everybody who was of any note made it a practice to visit the place regularly and buy some new high-priced piece of delicate china.

Bentley wrote to Wedgwood and told him of the need

for these imitation Greek vases in his showrooms. Everybody was asking for them.

These vases were adorned with graceful figures of men and women modelled in relief. To make them, Wedgwood found it necessary to employ expert modellers and artists. He still carried on his own experiments, though, shaping, modelling, firing, and painting new designs for vessels. The more he worked at the 'wheel,' the more fascinated he became with his work. He once wrote in a letter to Bentley, "Whoever tastes a little of the fruits of vase-making will afterwards spare no costs or pains to have a full meal."

We have not said much about Wedgwood's health in the last few pages, but perhaps that is because he stoically carried on, year in, year out, without complaint. Nevertheless, he had never ridded himself of the after-effects of his childhood illness of smallpox. His knee had always been a source of trouble to him, but now it was getting worse. The disease was spreading, and the pains were causing him to lose his bodily strength. At length, after many consultations with the doctor, it was decided that the leg must be amputated if his life was to be saved.

Any operation in those days was a very unpleasant affair for the patient. There were no hospitals, and anaesthetics had not been discovered. One had to bear the agony of sitting and watching the doctor carry out his task. It is recorded that Wedgwood sat in his kitchen chair without a groan or murmur, except to pass a joke with the doctor, throughout the operation. He laughingly said to the doctor, "We must call this day St Amputation Day," and each time the anniversary of this day came round he was said to have repeated his little joke to his friends.

As soon as he could get about again after the operation, he was back in the works at his beloved bench. The name of Wedgwood was now world-famous. Even Royalty was using his china-ware. Other manufacturers were becoming jealous of his good name, and some tried to copy his pottery by forging his trade-marks. But they failed lamentably. The buyers could always tell the difference between the fakes and the genuine articles. These manufacturers had not the knowledge of Wedgwood's clay mixtures to make accurate copies of his work.

The next triumph in Wedgwood's career as a master potter was conveyed to him in a letter from Bentley.

> My good friend and partner [he wrote], you will no doubt be gratified and delighted to hear that her Gracious Majesty, Catherine II, Empress of Russia, has been favourably impressed with examples of our ware which she has seen in the residence of the British Ambassador there. As a result she has instructed this same Ambassador to obtain for her a special dinner-service for use at State banquets in the Imperial Palace.

The letter continued with instructions as to how the Empress desired the service to be made. Each plate, dish, and jug was to be decorated with painted scenes of various parts of England, a country which she adored and wished to know more about. She had conceived the idea that this dinner-service would be an excellent way of seeing England in pictures.

This order came as a great honour to Wedgwood, and he decided to make the service a masterpiece of his craft. Much work had to be done in preparing special designs, and the painted scenes presented some difficulty. How was he going to obtain enough different pictures to cover the numerous pieces required for the complete set? He solved this problem by employing several eminent artists to travel over England to make drawings of country mansions, river- and landscape-scenes, and even scenes of industrial life, such as pit-heads showing the miners going to work, fishermen unloading their catches, masons erecting great buildings, and so on.

The service took over a year to make, and contained nearly 1300 separate pieces of china. It cost the Empress more than three thousand pounds, but she was so delighted

with it that it was kept unused, in case any pieces got broken, in a show-room at the palace for all her visitors to admire.

But even this example of Wedgwood's great skill as a craftsman was superseded by a piece of work which he carried out later. This was his work of copying the famous Portland Vase. This vase was an unusual and beautiful specimen of the work of an ancient Greek sculptor.

THE PORTLAND VASE

It had recently been unearthed from among some Grecian ruins and brought to England by the Duke of Portland, hence its name. The surface of the vase was of a very delicate blue colour surmounted with beautiful sculptured human figures carved in a milky white stone. It was thought that the sculptor must have used a very unusual piece of stone or marble, for the white figures seemed to emerge from the blue ground as from one piece. When Wedgwood first saw it he was so struck by its beauty that he vowed he would make an attempt to copy it faithfully. The main difficulty was to obtain the correct mixings of clay to get the colours of the original. He saw the Duke of Portland and persuaded him to lend him the original vase. He must have pleaded with the Duke very strongly, for it was worth a great amount of money, and the slightest misfortune befalling it would have ruined its value.

The work of copying proved to be very difficult and slow. Many times the work had to be abandoned, when in an advanced stage, because of some slight difference from the original detected in it. Twice Wedgwood finished copies, but he was not satisfied with their accuracy; so each time, with great determination and patience, he started all over again. Eventually he was rewarded for his pains. The perfect copy was completed. Compliments and praise poured in from all kinds of people when they heard of this great masterpiece of craftsmanship. The Duke of Portland said that he could not distinguish it from the original, which was very great praise indeed.

This great achievement settled Wedgwood's fame as the cleverest potter of all time, and his name as a craftsman has passed down to the present day through his works. People still associate any pottery after the style of the Portland Vase with his name and call it "Wedgwood Ware."

The master potter died in the year 1795 at the age of sixty-five, after having completed a full and useful life of glorious achievements in his craft. The pottery to which he gave his name nearly two hundred years ago is in being to this day.

VIII

SIR RICHARD ARKWRIGHT
Mechanical Engineer

Two days before Christmas in the year 1732 there was born in a humble cottage in the town of Preston, Lanca-

SIR RICHARD ARKWRIGHT

shire, a baby boy. He was given the name of Richard Arkwright—a name which was destined to become famous in the history of England.

Richard was the thirteenth child of his parents, and as they were only poor working people you can understand how difficult it must have been to buy enough food and clothing for such a large family out of the meagre wages of Mr Arkwright. What a job it must have been for Mrs Arkwright to provide a dinner each day for fifteen hungry mouths when she could only spare a few coppers for the food!

But there were so many families living at that time in similar circumstances that Richard's home was no poorer than the majority of others in Preston. All the working people found it a hard struggle to live. Long hours each day they toiled, with very little time to spare for leisure. There were no schools for the children, who often started working before they were nine years old. If we were suddenly put to live as these people did we should, without doubt, find life very difficult; but as they had never known anything better, they took little notice of their hardships.

Richard grew up none the worse for living in such poor circumstances. He was healthy, bright, and intelligent, and was possessed of an inquiring mind. From a very early age he showed great determination to succeed in life and was always alert to gather any knowledge which might prove useful to him later on.

Richard had an uncle of the same name living near by who was fortunate enough to be able to read and write— a very unusual accomplishment for an ordinary person in those days. Young Richard thought his uncle a very clever man because he could read, and he resolved to learn to do the same things as soon as he got the opportunity.

One day Uncle Richard came to the house to read a letter for Richard's mother. She had received it but could not read it. Young Richard listened very intently while his uncle slowly read out the words contained in the letter, and afterwards asked:

"Uncle, will you teach me to read and write as well as you can? I would then be able to read things for Mother."

"Of course I will teach you if you want to learn," replied the uncle. "But it is not often that a child so young as you is anxious to learn lessons. Anyway, I shall come round once a week and give you a lesson, and we shall see how long you keep them up."

Uncle Richard did not expect the boy to keep on the lessons for long; he thought Richard would soon find learning to read very dull and uninteresting. But he was greatly mistaken, for whenever after that he came round to the house to give a lesson, Richard was always ready and eager to learn more about reading and writing. The boy progressed in his studies rapidly and soon began to read very well. In this way Richard was able to obtain a certain standard of education which was denied to boys of his class in those days.

When Richard was old enough to start work, his father was anxious to find him a better job than most boys had. He hoped that Richard, being clever enough to be able to read and write, would be able to work at something better than labouring in the coal-mine or weaving on the loom. He thought the boy deserved an occupation more suited to an educated person. Eventually he got him apprenticed to a hairdresser named Nicholson, who had a tiny shop in Preston.

Richard liked the work very well. The job was cleaner and more pleasant than most others, and the hours of working were shorter. During his apprenticeship Richard still pursued his reading- and writing-lessons at an evening school. For these lessons he had to pay twopence a week, and as he saved the money out of his small wages, you can be sure that he was very keen to improve his learning. Most boys would have thought it a waste to use money in such a way, but not so Richard. He realized that if he was to get on in the world he must have some education.

As soon as his years of apprenticeship were over and he had learnt to be a good hairdresser, Richard moved to the town of Bolton to work for a new master. He was restless, though, in this job. He wanted to get on in life. Working for another master seemed a great drudgery to him. He had made up his mind to found a business of his own some day and be his own master. But one needed money to start a business, and although he was careful to save part of his small wages each week, Richard could see that it would take him years to collect all the money he needed.

Then in 1755 he married the daughter of one Robert Hall, a schoolmaster of Bolton. Luckily his wife had a little money of her own at the time of the marriage, and five years later, when he had saved enough, Richard started his first hairdressing-shop. This new business quickly began to prosper and bring in a good living each week, but Richard was still impatient to get on and make money rapidly. So within a year of opening his first shop, he took over a larger one in a more prosperous part of the town. Here again his business flourished, but still he was not satisfied with the rate of his progress.

LADIES' WIGS IN THE EIGHTEENTH CENTURY

He said to his wife:

"The work of cutting hair is too hard, and the profits are too small for my liking. I want to earn much more money than I am doing now, but I do not know what I could do to pay me more."

"Why not try wig-making?" queried his wife after some thought. "Wigs are fashionable, and people will pay good prices for well-made ones. You could get somebody to help you, and then you should get good profits from this work."

Richard thought carefully about this suggestion. It seemed a good idea. To make wigs he would need quantities of human hair, special dyes, and an experienced wig-maker to do the work. He decided to try out his wife's suggestion. He worked out the plans for his new business and engaged a wig-maker named Leigh to do the work for him. Leigh was a skilful workman, and the strong wigs he made found a ready sale.

Richard found that the demands for his wigs were too great for the amount of hair he could obtain in and round Bolton, so he began to spend his time travelling round the country visiting 'hiring-fairs.'

'Hiring-fairs' were held in all the market towns in those days, so that farmers could come into the town and choose the labourers and serving-maids they would need to work for them during the next year. The day on which a 'hiring-fair' was held was a day of festivity for the inhabitants. The market square would be thronged with people laughing and singing, and the farmers would mix with them and make arrangements with those workmen they wanted to employ.

Richard Arkwright would also mix with the throng of people and would bargain with one girl after another for their unwanted locks of hair. Then home he would go after the fair, with a goodly parcel of human hair for Leigh, his workman, to make up into wigs.

At one of these fairs Arkwright had a great stroke of luck. He learned from a man, who had over-feasted and was not quite sober, a closely guarded secret of a very valuable chemical dye for colouring hair. With his usual keenness for business he soon made use of this secret he had acquired. He began to dye the hair he bought with this new chemical and to sell the products to other wig-makers. As the dye gave excellent and lasting colours to the hair, the wig-makers were anxious to buy it, and Arkwright was soon reaping good profits.

But his alert mind was now turning towards other things. His journeys round the country caused him to meet many people engaged in the work of spinning and weaving, and, being inquisitive by nature, he began to take a great interest in the new inventions of weaving-machines which everybody was talking about. The weavers and spinners were getting worried. Until now they had always spun and woven their cloths on their little hand-wheels and looms, and now machines were being invented which would do the work for them. They were saying:

"These new-fangled monsters of machines will do our work for us, and we shall soon be unemployed and then we shall starve. The invention of these machines is not good for us."

They were afraid that the coming of the machines would put an end to their means of livelihood. But not so Arkwright. He could see that these machines were to be the means of doing the spinning and weaving in the future, and he could see that the first men who made use of them would reap rich rewards. He decided to learn as much about them as he could and to find out if he could use his wits in this direction.

He studied the inventions which had already become known. John Kay, a watch-maker of Warrington, had patented, some years previously, a flying shuttle for the weaving-loom. This shuttle had made the work of weaving much quicker, and more cloth could be woven with it by one man than could be done by three or four men on hand-looms. This shuttle did the work so fast that the spinners could not spin their yarns fast enough to keep the weaver supplied, and various inventors began to try to think of ways of speeding up the work of spinning.

In 1767 James Hargreaves, a carpenter of Blackburn, invented and built a machine which was called the spinning-jenny. This machine made it possible to spin twenty or thirty threads in the time taken to spin one thread by hand. But this machine had a great fault. It could only spin threads which were strong enough to use as the cross-threads, or weft, as they are called, of a piece of cloth, and the long, or warp, threads still had to be spun by hand.

By this time, though, Arkwright had worked out an idea for a spinning-frame, and he was anxious to build a model of it. He told his wife of his idea and said to her:

"In order to make my spinning-frame I must have time to work, so I shall have to give up my business. I shall also have to get a man to help me who is skilled in metal-working to make the parts for me."

His wife was aghast when she heard this. She exclaimed:

"What a ridiculous idea! And how are we going to get a living if you give up your work to play about with this foolish idea. You will do far better to stick to your rightful business."

"But can you not see that we shall make a fortune if my machine works? All the yarn used in the country will be spun on my machines. I shall become a rich man in a very short time," replied Arkwright with conviction.

"But what will happen if your machine does not work? You will then have no business and no money, and we shall starve," answered Mrs Arkwright.

But Arkwright was convinced that his idea would work. He carried out his intentions against all the pleadings of his wife. He gave up his business and employed John Kay, the inventor of the flying shuttle, to help him "bend some wires and turn some pieces of brass."

Between them they constructed some wooden models of Arkwright's idea, which worked well enough to convince the inventor that a large spinning-frame built on the same lines would solve the problem of spinning many strong threads simultaneously and quickly.

So now Arkwright and Kay set to work to build a full-sized spinning-frame. As they did not want the news of their work to leak out, in case somebody stole the invention from them, they worked secretly in the parlour of a house belonging to the Free Grammar School at Preston. A friend of Arkwright's named John Smalley gave them the use of the room. The house was enclosed by a garden well filled with trees and bushes, so they could work secretly without fear of prying eyes round them.

They constructed the spinning-frame in good time, but the secrecy of their methods aroused the suspicions of the people who were living near. They were curious to know what was going on in the house. Some said that they were practising witchcraft. One woman frightened her neighbours by saying:

"Strange noises of a queer humming nature do I hear coming from that house. Those men

ARKWRIGHT'S SPINNING-FRAME

are up to no good. I do believe those sounds are of Satan tuning up his bagpipes while those wicked men dance to the tune."

People began to get afraid to pass the house, so dreadful were the rumours that were spreading round. They talked of nothing but the weird humming noises that could be heard all day long coming from the place. So great did everybody's fear become that some suggested breaking into the house to settle their doubts once and for all.

But Arkwright and Kay persevered. Arkwright was by

now in dire straits. His money had practically gone, his clothes were in rags, and he had little food. He began to wonder if his wife had been right after all—if he would have done better to have kept on his hairdressing-business and left his invention alone.

Time and time again the two men dismantled their spinning-frame because it did not work well enough to satisfy Arkwright. Each time it was assembled again new improvements were added to it.

Then at last, after having given the machine a thorough test, the two men decided that it worked well enough to use commercially. It proved to be so much superior to Hargreaves' spinning-jenny that it could spin any number of threads at once, making them fine and strong enough to use for both the weft and warp threads of a length of cloth. Although reduced to a sad state of poverty, Arkwright had now been rewarded for his persistence in his idea. He had succeeded in constructing the first satisfactory spinning-frame.

The first thing that Arkwright did when he was certain that his machine worked well was to patent it, so that others could not steal his idea and make use of it for their own profit. This he did in the year 1769, two years after he had started his experiments.

But now came the problem as to how to use the spinning-frame so as to make profits from it. A spinning-mill would have to be built to produce the yarn from his machines. But Arkwright was afraid to work his machine publicly in Lancashire, as the people were so antagonistic to such things, and it was more than likely that they would smash it up as soon as they saw it, as they once did to a spinning-jenny of Hargreaves'.

He could not risk the smashing up of his beloved machine by an angry mob, so he had to find some other part of the country where he could erect his mill in safety.

Finally he decided to build the mill in Nottingham, a town where much spinning and weaving of stockings was carried on. Arkwright's friend, John Smalley, provided the money and went with him to Nottingham as a partner in the business, while Kay went as a bonded workman.

So, after some months, the mill started to produce finely spun yarn. Horses were used to turn the wheels of the machines, and work went ahead at a good pace. As the spinning-frames did their work they gave off a sound similar to the whistling of a thrush, and consequently people nicknamed them "throstle-frames."

But after the mill had been working a few weeks money ran short again. Arkwright began to worry about it. He said to his partner:

"John, I am afraid we shall not be able to carry on much longer. The money has nearly gone, debts are piling up, and we shall soon be unable to feed the horses and pay the men. What are we to do about it? It will kill me to give up my work now that I have succeeded so far."

Smalley thought the matter over and then said to Arkwright:

"We must get the money from somewhere to keep the mill going. If we can carry on for a year or so we shall then begin to reap in the profits. There will be more buyers of our yarn as they get to hear of us and our work. Anyway, we cannot let your invention rust and you starve now that you have succeeded in bringing it to such a state of perfection. Do not let us give up hope yet. I know a rich manufacturer who may be interested enough in the idea to lend us some money. I will make the journey to see him."

The man Smalley referred to was one Jedediah Strutt, who lived in Derbyshire. Strutt was interested in inventions and had himself invented a ribbing-machine for weaving stockings in a special manner.

Smalley went to see him and convinced him that it would be worth his while to examine Arkwright's spinning-frame, so Strutt journeyed back to Nottingham with him.

Arkwright demonstrated the spinning-frame to Mr Strutt, who made a careful examination of the way it worked. Afterwards he said to Arkwright:

"To me your spinning-frame seems to have great possibilities of success, and I shall be ready to help you with money to carry on the good work. But you must start manufacturing yarn on a much larger scale than you are doing at present in order to bring in the profits quickly."

JEDEDIAH STRUTT
By courtesy of the English Sewing Cotton Co., Ltd.

Arkwright was delighted. He would now be able to carry on working with his machines, altering and improving them. He had feared that he would have to go back to his old work of hairdressing, but now new hope shone in his eyes.

A partnership was arranged between Arkwright and Strutt, and eventually, in 1771, a large mill, equipped with a number of Arkwright's spinning-frames, was erected at a small town called Cromford, in Derbyshire, near to Mr Strutt's home. This time the frames were driven by water-wheels, a new method thought of by Arkwright as being much less expensive than horse-power. The mill was built on the side of a valley near a natural water-spring, the water of which was so warm that it never froze. The warmness of the water allowed Arkwright's water-wheels to keep turning all the year round, so that there would be no stoppage to the machinery.

But fresh difficulties soon came in the way of Arkwright's progress. His machines had begun to spin yarn

ARKWRIGHT'S WATER-FRAME

at a fast pace, and now all that was needed to bring in the profits so long waited for was to be able to sell the finished yarn. But the Lancashire manufacturers could not be persuaded to purchase anything which had been made on the machines they hated, even if it was cheaper and better than that made by hand.

This trouble came as another great blow to Arkwright. It was useless to spin fine yarn if nobody would buy it. Eventually Strutt thought of an idea. He said to the worried Arkwright:

"If nobody will buy our yarn, let us use it ourselves. We will weave it into stockings and sell them instead of the yarn."

So the partners began to weave stockings, which, being

much smoother in texture and neater in appearance than those woven by hand, found a ready sale.

For all the setbacks to his initiative Arkwright continued to experiment with his spinning-frames and improve upon them. In the year 1773 he discovered certain improvements which allowed his frames to spin cotton thread strong enough to make calico solely from cotton instead of using linen-warp threads, as was done by other weavers.

These new cloths soon met with great demand, as they were more finely woven and cheaper than any others that could be bought.

Success seemed to be on its way to Arkwright at last. Sales were increasing rapidly. Then another severe blow fell on the business.

The manufacturers of Lancashire began to fear they would lose their trade and looked for ways to put a stop to Arkwright's progress. They soon discovered that there was an old Act of Parliament which forbade anyone to make cloth solely from cotton without paying a double tax on it. They quickly combined together and got the Government to enforce the law, so that Arkwright had to pay the extra tax on his goods. No longer could he sell his cloths cheaply as before, and naturally the sales began to fall off.

But he persevered. He had not lost his determination to succeed, and he started, with the aid of Strutt and other influential men, to persuade the Government to take the tax off cotton goods. After many setbacks he eventually succeeded in getting an Act passed in the year 1774 exempting from tax all "new stuffs wholly made from raw cotton."

By this time, though, more than £12,000 had been spent by Arkwright, Smalley, and Strutt between them in perfecting the spinning-frames, and very little returns had they received for their labours and money. But the passing of the new Act altered all this. The business began to develop rapidly. Sales increased at a tremendous pace. People were just beginning to realize the value of Arkwright's spinning-frames.

Then, in the year 1775, Arkwright patented an invention of a machine which did various jobs in the cotton-factory, and which he called a "carding, drawing, and roving machine for use in preparing silk, cotton, flax, and wool for spinning."

His energies were boundless. He organized the working of the machines and taught the workmen how to use them. He was continually thinking out new ideas for improving his machines.

The cotton-factory at Cromford became one of the wonders of the age. There was a constant stream of visitors to see the marvellous new machines working, and most of them bought a dozen or two pairs of stockings to take home with them as a memento of their visit. Everybody was talking about Arkwright's great inventions. He was becoming known throughout the land.

One famous man of the time, named Dr Erasmus Darwin, visited the factory and then went home and wrote a poem about what he saw. This is a part of what he wrote:

First, with nice eye, emerging Naiads cull
From leathery pods the vegetable wool,
With wiry teeth revolving cards release
The tangled knots and smooth the ravelled fleece:
Next moves the iron hand with fingers fine,
Combs the wide card and forms the eternal line;
Slow with soft lips the whirling can acquires
The tender skeins, and wraps in rising spires:
With quickened pace successive rollers move,
And these retain, and those extend, the rove;
Then fly the spokes, the rapid axles glow,
While slowly circumvolves the labouring wheel below.

But with Arkwright's rise to fame came more trouble. Some of the visitors to his factory were rival manufacturers who made a study of his machines and then went away to copy them and use them in their own factories. His workmen were continually being bribed to go and work for the other manufacturers, who did not know how to use the machines. They carried all this out in face of the fact that Arkwright's machines were patented and by law nobody else was allowed to construct or use them without Arkwright's permission.

To some honest manufacturers Arkwright did grant the right to build and use his machines for certain sums of money, but the others, who had paid nothing for the privilege, were beginning to steal some of his profits by selling similar goods. Arkwright decided that it was time to put a stop to this. So, in the year 1781, he had nine manufacturers summoned in Court for stealing his patents and using his inventions for profit without permission. Here was an opportunity for the Lancashire cotton-manufacturers to take their revenge on Arkwright, whom they hated intensely. They banded themselves together, went to Court to give evidence in the case, and did their best to make the Court believe that Arkwright did not really invent the machines he had patented. They said that he had copied other inventors' ideas and made use of them for his own purpose. So convincing was their evidence that Arkwright lost the case, and the manufacturers were still at liberty to use his machines without paying for the privilege.

Losing this case hurt Arkwright's pride greatly. He would now be looked upon as a fraud. That was all the gratitude he got after spending the best years of his life in inventing and perfecting machines to be used for the benefit of his fellow-men. It was not so much the loss of trade, which was sure to come as other manufacturers made more of his stuff, that hurt his pride, but more that people would not now believe that he was the inventor of these wonderful machines. In order to try to clear his character he published a pamphlet telling the story of the trials and hardships he had endured while working on his inventions. He also thought of applying to Parliament to see if they would grant him his patent rights back.

Eventually, in the year 1785, he succeeded in opening a new trial to try to get the protection of his patents again. During the trial it was learned, much to Arkwright's distress, that his machines were being worked by more than thirty thousand workmen in factories of manufacturers who had stolen his inventions. That meant that thousands of pounds in profits, which rightly belonged to him, were going into the pockets of other manufacturers every week. In spite of the evidence brought in his favour, Arkwright again lost the case. The rival manufacturers, by reason of the many falsehoods they told in the witness-box, convinced the judge that Arkwright was the untruthful one ! 'The judge told Arkwright, "Right from the start of the trial you have told a pack of lies, and you have not a leg to stand on."

But the prosperity of Arkwright's factory was not held up as a result of the trial. He had obtained a good lead over the other manufacturers during the years before they stole his patents, and his business had become too well established to lose its trade now. People knew that the cotton goods made at Arkwright's factory were the best of their kind and they continued to buy them.

So rapidly did the business grow that the work of spinning and weaving soon became more than the factory at Cromford could manage, so Arkwright began to erect further mills in other parts of Derbyshire and in Lancashire.

In Lancashire he still received occasional trouble at the

hands of some of the old-fashioned spinners and weavers. They still thought that the machines were evil monsters which would put them out of work, and sometimes they would burn one of Arkwright's newly erected factories to the ground in their anger.

For all these expensive and upsetting incidents, Arkwright's business grew from strength to strength, and he was on the way towards amassing a great fortune well deserved after his years of intense labour. He was now regarded as the greatest cotton-manufacturer in the country, and his name had become famous.

His newly acquired fortune and fame did not make any change in his mode of living, though. He still continued to work as hard as he did in his younger days, starting each day soon after five o'clock in the morning and never finishing until about nine o'clock at night. His energy and enthusiasm for work would scarcely allow him a minute's rest. He was always doing something.

He was always the first cotton-manufacturer to adopt new ideas and improvements to his factories if he thought them worth while, and in 1790 he used one of James Watt's first steam-engines to drive the machines in one of his mills.

Four years previously, in 1786, he had been made a knight by King George III, and in the following year he was appointed to the honoured position of High Sheriff of Derbyshire.

Sir Richard Arkwright, the hairdresser's apprentice who had, by perseverance and endeavour, risen to be the greatest cotton-manufacturer in England, ended his busy and productive life on the third of August, 1792, at the age of sixty.

IX

JAMES WATT

Mathematical-instrument Maker

IN the year 1736 there was living and working in the busy little fishing-town of Greenock, on the River Clyde, one Thomas Watt, who carried on the business of carpenter and shipwright. His little workshop was situated on the quay, so that he and his workmen might do any repairs to the fishermen's boats quickly to avoid delaying the fishermen any longer than was necessary between trips out to sea. As his was the only workshop of its kind in the town, many and varied

JAMES WATT
National Portrait Gallery

were the jobs to be carried out. He would replace deckplanks when they had rotted or masts which had been smashed in heavy gales, and he would even undertake to repair the ship's instruments when they went wrong, as there was no one else who could manage such work. Consequently, as his experience grew, he learned much about many kinds of practical work as well as that of

153

wood-working. To carry out such a variety of work to the complete satisfaction of the local fishermen and towns-people, Mr Watt must have been a very skilful and adaptable workman.

By the side of this busy workshop he also carried on a little business as ship's chandler. There could be obtained any requisites necessary for a trip out to sea. On entering the shop one would see, stacked on shelves, on the counter, on the floor, and perhaps also hanging from the ceiling, a miscellaneous array of such fishing-necessities as food-stuffs, stoves, oil, lamps, candles, rope, hooks, twine, and navigation instruments. Anything the fishermen might require quickly Thomas Watt would stock.

On June 19 of this year a son, who was destined to become known as the famous James Watt, the inventor and builder of the first satisfactory steam-engine, was born into the home of this shipwright.

James grew up to be a weakly and ailing child, often confined to his home or bed with childish ailments, too delicate to play the boisterous games indulged in by the other boys of his age who lived near him. He was so weakly that he was afraid to stay out in the evenings with the other boys in case he got hurt, and so he looked for other things to amuse him in his spare time. He spent many hours in and round his father's workshop, taking a great interest in watching the men carry out the repairs to the ships.

Then, on his tenth birthday, among his many presents, he received some mechanical toys sent to him by one of his aunts. He quickly became very interested in these, finding out how they worked and taking them to pieces to see how they had been made. He found it an exciting and absorbing hobby to take two or three toys to pieces and, from these pieces, try to build an entirely new kind of working toy. He became so interested in this hobby that his father allowed him to use some of the tools in the workshop, and from that time he spent many hours at his father's bench working with any odd scraps of wood and metal which he found lying about. He began to become quite a clever worker in the use of tools, and at quite an early age he could use a plane, saw, or file as well as many men.

When he was at home in the evenings, after the workshop had been locked up for the day, he would spend much time sitting and thinking of ways in which he could improve his toys or invent new ones. His parents could not understand him at these times and took him to be just a lazy person with nothing better to do than to mope in front of the fire.

One day the aunt who had sent him the toys was staying at James's home, and she became quite cross seeing him there saying nothing, but just staring before him at the kettle boiling on the hob. Unable to control her anger, she sharply reprimanded James, saying:

"James, I never saw such an idle boy as you are. Take a book to read, or employ yourself usefully. For the last hour you have not spoken one word, but have sat there taking the lid off the kettle and putting it on again, holding now a cup, now a silver spoon over the steam, watching how it has risen from the spout, and catching and counting the drops it falls into."

James mumbled something about being sorry, but he did not cease to wonder about the steam that was continually rising from the kettle and dispersing in the air. He noticed that the steam kept trying to push the kettle-lid off and that it changed back into water when it was caught in the silver spoon. He felt that some use could be made of this wasted steam, but he could not at this time see just how. It was not until some years later that he answered this question for himself.

As he grew older he had to start working, and his father, noticing how clever he was with his hands, decided to let him become a mathematical-instrument maker. To make delicate instruments one has to be an extremely accurate and skilful worker, and Watt's father rightly thought that he would become a good one. He started as a workman in his father's shop, repairing the instruments brought in from the local ships, and, after a year or two at this, his health began to improve. During his nightly strolls along the quay he found an interest in watching and understanding the stars. As he was always eager to know more about anything in which he took an interest, he bought and read books on the subject and studied the instruments used for measuring them. This hobby helped him considerably in his own work, as he learned much more about the mathematical instruments used in astronomy.

Eventually he began to feel that he wanted to learn more about his work than was possible in his father's tiny repair-shop; so one day he spoke to his father about it.

"Father, I want to learn more about my work by studying and making the instruments used on the great ships, none of which ever come to Greenock. How can I do so?"

His father replied, "Only by securing a post in the workshop of a maker of these large instruments, such as would be found in great cities like Edinburgh, and that is a long way to travel alone."

And so it was in those days, with only narrow winding lanes as roads and only horseback as a means of travel. For a young man who had never before left his home town it would be a very great adventure to travel such a distance alone. Nevertheless, James was determined to do something about it, and after a few days he approached his father about it again.

"Father," he said resolutely, but at the same time fearing for what his father's answer might be, "I am anxious to improve my knowledge. May I make the journey to the city of Edinburgh and there try my fortune?"

Although the father was sad at the thought of losing his son he decided to let him go, as James seemed so determined about it. So, equipped with food, a horse, and a little money, he set off across Scotland to Edinburgh. But in Edinburgh, after many days' search and many disappointments, he could find no suitable master with whom he could obtain work. He was told by six ships' captains whom he asked that the only place to find work in his trade was in London. Now from Edinburgh to London was a much longer journey than that which he had already made, but, undaunted by his failure, he set off with the remainder of the money his father had given him. After a long and arduous journey on horseback he arrived in London, only to find that more troubles were awaiting him.

For a long time he could get no suitable employment there, and he found it very difficult to live on the little money he had left. Eventually he met an instrument-maker who was willing to teach him the trade thoroughly, but in return he demanded a sum of twenty guineas as a premium. Not having the money himself, he wrote home to his father for it. Although the little business at Greenock was always busy, it was too small to bring in a large profit; but the shipwright managed to collect enough money together to send off the required premium to his son.

So James started work at a wage of eight shillings a week. This wage was too small for him to live on, and so, even though his father continued to send him small amounts when he could spare them, James had to earn a few extra shillings by doing instrument- and watch-repairs in his lodgings at night after he had finished his day's work for his master.

These long hours of work and weeks without much food soon made him ill again, and, finding that he could carry on no longer in the smoky atmosphere of London, he packed up his things and returned home to Greenock. There, he spent a few months resting to recover his health: but he could not continue long without earning something, so he gathered some tools together and set off to Glasgow, deciding to set up in business as an instrument-maker. But here again he found trouble. The workmen already trading in the city would not allow him to start another business, as it meant less trade for them. So he found himself still in the dilemma of not knowing how to earn a living.

After a time he became friendly with a professor at Glasgow University, who, hearing of his plight, found him a room inside the University where he could work at his trade. He began to repair instruments, watches, or mechanical tools and to do any work by which he could earn a living. In whatever spare time he had he would make scientific instruments in the hope that he would be able to sell them.

The professors used to watch him at work, and so impressed were they on seeing his skilful fingers manipulate and assemble the pieces of metal into a delicate and accurate instrument that they provided him with a shop within the University wherein he could display his wares for sale.

This shop did not prove to be at all profitable, and here again Watt found it difficult to earn enough to buy himself food and provide for his lodgings. Although he did not tell the professors of his dire need, they all knew about it, and during a talk one evening, one of their number suggested that Watt should use his abilities in working at something more profitable than making scientific instruments which nobody seemed to want.

"But what do you suggest?" asked Watt. "I have had no training in any other kind of work."

"There are many kinds of work. one can do if he is clever. with his hands," was the reply. "Why not try making simple musical instruments? Musical instruments would have a much readier sale than the kind you make."

"But I am deaf and do not understand a thing about music. I do not see how I can make accurate instruments if I do not understand or appreciate what they are supposed to do," said Watt.

"That need not deter you. You can learn how the notes on an instrument are produced scientifically without being a musician."

This conversation led Watt to buy books on the subject of musical-instrument making, and when he knew all he could learn about it, he set to work in his spare time constructing fiddles, flutes, and guitars. He managed to sell these, and this spare-time work—he would not give up his work of making scientific instruments—brought him in enough money to live fairly comfortably.

Seeing how successfully he was making these small instruments, one of the professors suggested that he should make a barrel-organ for him. Watt was not at all sure that he could manage this at first, but with his usual thoroughness he bought more books and learned as much as he could about organs. Then he set to work and designed an organ of which he first made a working model to test his design before embarking on a larger one. So pleased was he with its performance that instead of completing the small barrel-organ he improved upon his design and built a full-size finger-organ, which was judged by clever musicians to be an excellent instrument.

About this time various other scientists were trying to make use of steam for working engines to pump water out of coal- and tin-mines.

A Frenchman, Dr Papin, was the first man who really

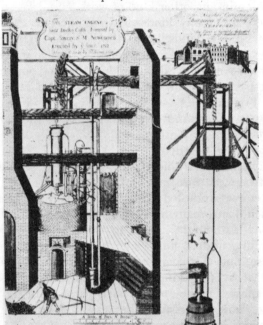

NEWCOMEN'S ATMOSPHERIC ENGINE
From an engraving in the Science Museum, South Kensington, London

used steam to work a pump which had been previously worked by hand, but his engine was costly and not very successful. Then another inventor, named Savery, built a very complicated steam-pump over his mine, but this proved to be useless and was abandoned.

One Thomas Newcomen saw this pump of Savery's, studied its construction, and from the knowledge he had gained, invented a better one. Although it was an improvement on the previous engines and many coal-owners had similar ones erected over their mines, this type of pump was not really very good. The coal-owners certainly found that their pumps managed to draw off the water from the mines, but they were costly to run and often broke down. Nevertheless, a considerable number of Newcomen's pumps were erected and used in various parts of the country for want of something better.

James Watt had never forgotten his boyish dreams about the possibilities of using steam to do work, so when he heard of Newcomen's engine, he became anxious to experiment again with steam. To see for himself the worth of these pumps of Newcomen's, about which he had heard such wonderful stories, he went to the trouble of obtaining a model of one. He experimented with it in his little workshop and found that, although it did work, it wasted a lot of steam in the process. The result was that he started thinking of ways in which he could make the engine more powerful and yet use less steam. He tried many experiments, failing many times, but eventually he built a model of an engine which was far more successful than any of the previous ones.

Nevertheless, he was far from satisfied with it, and he kept altering the design and making improvements to various parts. This work became so intensely interesting to him that he began to spend most of his time at it, neglecting his main work of instrument-making. His money began to run short, but he could not leave his experiments, as it was now his cherished dream to build the perfect steam-engine.

Professor Black, a very great friend of Watt's and a frequent visitor to his workshop, knew of his want of money and tried to think of ways by which he could help him. He knew that it would be useless trying to persuade

Watt to resume his former work, so he looked for some one who could finance him in his experiments.

One evening the professor stood watching Watt at work when he suddenly said, "How would you like to build a full-size steam-engine over a coal-mine?"

"That is my ambition," replied Watt. "But how is it possible without money to buy materials and pay workmen? I must also find a mine-owner who will have faith in the power of my engine so that I may make use of his mine-head for erecting it."

"I have been discussing your model engine with a friend of mine—an influential coal-owner—and I think I have interested him sufficiently to make him want to see it working," said the professor in a quiet voice. "He already has a Newcomen engine working at one of his mines, but he is far from satisfied with its capabilities Therefore, if you can construct a satisfactory model of your engine including the improvements of your latest experiments, I will show it to him. We may then persuade him to pay for one to be built at his mine. Then, if you are successful and get it working, orders will come in for others."

Watt took Professor Black's advice and began to build his new model, but his funds were so low that he had to find other work to do long before the engine was finished. He had already acquired a good knowledge of surveying through reading books on the subject, so, deciding that it was a better business than the one he was engaged in, he began work as a surveyor of canals and building-land. This brought him in enough money to live on, and did not allow him much time to work on his beloved engine.

However, during any spare hour he would do a little more to it until at last it was finished and working satisfactorily. As its design was entirely different from the engines of the other inventors, he patented it so that no one could steal his ideas.

He then got Professor Black to arrange a meeting with the coal-owner. This man was extremely pleased with

EARLY WATT PUMPING-ENGINE, 1777
From the remains in the Science Museum, South Kensington, London

the engine when he saw it working in Watt's workshop, and he said, "Mr Watt, I will make you a proposition. If you will erect a large engine over one of my mines I will provide you with the money you require to buy materials and pay workmen. Then, if it works successfully, you must let me become your partner in making and selling others."

Watt was delighted with this offer and immediately

set off to the mine to superintend the building of his great engine. His new-found happiness was soon upset, though. He found that the work of building a large engine .was much more difficult than that of building a model. He was unable to obtain good enough workmen, and continually he was making them alter work which they had done badly. These alterations cost time and trouble, and he spent many sleepless nights wondering if, when all the bother of building was over, the engine would turn out a success or failure. You could never tell what might happen with such bad workmen as these.

When the time came for the engine's first trial, Watt nervously lit the fire beneath, which was to convert the water in the boiler into steam. Everybody who had anything at all to do with the job waited impatiently for the steam to rise. Then Watt noticed that the steam was beginning to leak from between the piston and cylinder. This was sufficient to make the whole experiment hopeless, as Watt quickly saw. Immediately he realized with a pang of despair that the cylinder had been made carelessly and the piston had not been fitted· accurately. As a temporary measure he tried packing the faulty spaces with cotton wool, but it was useless. The engine would not work, and the pumps remained idle. The trial had to be abandoned and Watt then tried to get better cylinders made, but without avail. The workmen, with their clumsy tools, were not capable enough.

Even these failures did not dishearten him, for he was sure that his engine would work if only he could get it made well enough. But the coal-owner was not so optimistic. He had spent more than he cared on it already. He was annoyed with Watt and would not lend him any more money, despite Watt's pleas that he could make the engine go if given time. Watt was again in debt himself, and he began to despair of ever finishing his engine. He said to a friend while in this melancholy mood, "Of all things in life, there is nothing more foolish than inventing." All the time, however, he continued to invent a great variety of articles, including a muffled furnace for melting metal and a new kind of telescope.

He gained no money from these small inventions, though, so he took charge of the building of a canal, hoping to work again at his engine in his spare time. His difficulty was still to get well-made parts for the engine, and, for the time being, he gave it up.

Some months later a friend, Dr Small, told him to go to Birmingham to see the wonderful metal-factories of a Mr Boulton, where it was possible that he would obtain good enough workmen to finish his engine. He was truly astounded at the cleverly constructed machinery which he saw on his visit to the factory, and during a talk with Boulton, induced him to have a model of his engine made by the best workmen. The fourteen-year patent on the engine was running out, so he knew he must be quick to get it working before other inventors had the opportunity of using his ideas.

The next difficulty which came Watt's way was that he lost his job as engineer-in-charge of the canal, as there was insufficient money to finish it. But although it was not realized at the time, this was really a piece of good fortune. Out of work and with no prospects, Watt visited Boulton again and interested him so much in his engine that they set up a partnership to make the engine afresh. Mr Boulton offered to supply workmen and machinery, and Watt was to be in charge of the work.

Matthew Boulton had a great personal interest in the engine, as the machinery in his factory was worked by water-wheels from the river, and when the water dried up in the hot summer months, horses had to be used, thus putting him to much expense.

L

Watt's first job in the new business was to have the old engine at the Scottish mine taken to pieces and sent down to Birmingham. It was rebuilt outside Boulton's factory. Then work was started on new pistons and cylinders.

BOULTON AND WATT ROTATIVE ENGINE, 1797
From the engine in Science Museum, South Kensington, London

Watt found the Birmingham workmen much more skilful than those he had employed before. The pistons were made to fit the cylinders, and all parts were made to work more accurately and smoothly. The engine was then given a trial, and, to the great joy of both Watt and Boulton, it worked successfully. Nevertheless, Watt was not satisfied yet, and after designing the engine again and improving various parts, he collected the best workmen he could find in Birmingham and had another engine built.

This engine worked marvellously, according to the standards of those days, and the fame of Boulton and Watt began to spread through the Midlands as inventors of a wonderful engine that would drive machinery, pump water, and do many other jobs with a great saving of time and labour. Soon many other inventors, knowing that the patent on the engine was due to expire shortly, began to steal ideas from it. Watt had much trouble about this and had to put his case before Parliament before the protection of the engine-design was extended for another period of years.

Orders for engines began to pour in from the Birmingham district, and a new factory had to be built to cope with the work. As time went by, orders were coming in from all over England and Scotland, and the names of Boulton and Watt became truly famous.

It was, of course, the increasing popularity of the steam-engine which led George Stephenson to build his locomotive, the "Rocket," the forerunner of great locomotives such as the "Coronation Scot" and the "Silver Jubilee."

After the business was well established, Watt decided to build himself a larger house in Birmingham than the one he was residing in at Harper's Hill, on the outskirts. He bought a plot of ground at Heathfield, a suburb of Birmingham, and had a fine house built by Samuel Wyatt, a well-known architect in those days. In this house was a small garret built under the roof which Watt converted into a workshop.

He really had no need to work now, as the sale of his steam-engines was bringing him plenty of money, but he found great pleasure in spending hours in his workshop. For the remainder of his life he was nearly always to be found at his bench inventing, constructing, and improving instruments and machines for the ultimate benefit of his fellow-men. One of his better-known inventions carried out in this garret was a machine which would make copies, in plaster of Paris, of sculptured figures and portraits.

WATT'S GARRET
From the original workshop in the Science Museum, South Kensington

When Watt died in 1819, after an extremely busy and useful life, his garret-workshop was left locked just as he had last left it, and so it remained for a number of years. When it was eventually reopened, one of the first visitors was Dr Smiles, who described it thus:

The room had been carefully locked up since Watt's death and had only been swept out once. Everything lay as he had left it. The piece of iron he was last employed in turning lay on the lathe. The ashes of the last fire were in

168

the grate, the last bit of coal was in the scuttle. The Dutch oven was in its place over the stove, and the frying-pan by which he cooked his meal was hanging by its accustomed nail. Many objects lay about or in the drawers, indicating the pursuits which had been interrupted by death—busts, medallions, and figures, waiting to be copied by the sculpture machine, many medallion moulds, a store of plaster of Paris, and a box of plaster casts from London, the contents of which had not been disturbed. Here are Watt's ladles for melting lead, his foot-rule, his glue-pot, his hammer. There are his compasses, quadrant glasses, scales, weights, and sundry boxes of mathematical instruments, once doubtless highly prized. In a little box, fitted with wooden cylinders mounted with paper and covered with figures, is what we suppose to be a model of a calculating-machine. On the shelves are minerals and chemicals in pots and jars, on which the dust of nearly half a century has settled. The moist substances have long since dried up, the putty has been turned to stone, and the paste to dust. On the shelf we come upon a withered bunch of grapes. Near at hand is the sculpture machine, on which he continued working till the end. Its wooden framing is worm-eaten and dropping into dust. But though the great workman has gone to rest and his handiwork is fast crumbling to decay, the spirit of his work, the thought which he put into his inventions, still survives and will probably continue to influence the destinies of his race for all time to come.

In 1924 the London Science Museum sent scientists to remove the garret from Birmingham and to place it on view in the museum so that everybody might see the room wherein the great craftsman and inventor did his work. The removal required much patience and skill on the part of the scientists, but eventually it was carried out successfully, and the room now stands in the museum, just as it was when Watt died. The shelves, well laden with tools and materials, the fireplace, the coal-hod containing its last piece of coal, the plates on which Watt had his meals—all were put back in their proper places. Watt's first steam-engine has also been removed to the same museum, reminding visitors of the great craftsman who succeeded in overcoming the trials of ill-health and hardship to give to the world one of the greatest. mechanical blessings it has ever known.

X

GEORGE STEPHENSON
Locomotive Engineer

ROBERT STEPHENSON and his wife and five children lived in a tiny cottage in the little village of Wylam, near Newcastle. The cottage was a humble, unhealthy home containing only two rooms with un-plastered ceilings and walls and damp clay floors. Mr Stephenson, like most men in the village, worked for long hours each day at the local coal-mine. His wages were only twelve shillings a week, and so you can under-stand that his family found it hard to get enough food to live on. But they did not complain. Mr and

GEORGE STEPHENSON
National Portrait Gallery

Mrs Stephenson were a hard-working couple and did all they could to keep their home happy and bright.

Mr Stephenson's job at the coal-mine was to keep stoking up the fire under the steam-engine which raised

171

the baskets of coal to the surface and pumped water out of the mine. The work was hard, but there were times between stokings when Mr Stephenson had nothing to do. Then he would feed the robins which used to settle on his engine in cold weather, or tell stories to the village children, who used to love to gather round him and listen to his exciting tales. All the children used to love 'Old Bob,' as they called him.

One of his most interested listeners when he was telling stories was his six-year-old son, George, who spent all his time at the mine. When his father was too busy to talk to him, George would go to the pit-head and watch the ropes from the engine haul up the great baskets of coal, and then help the men load the coal into the wagons which took it to the ships anchored in the river near by. George often used to walk by the side of one of the horses, holding its reins, as it hauled its heavy wagon along the wooden wagon-road.

George was a bright lad and was always asking his father about how the engine worked. This great steam-engine fascinated him, and he wanted to know all about it so that he could work it himself one day. He often used to say to his father, "When can I start work, Dad, and help earn money for Mother? I know a lot about your engine now, and I could help you work it." But his father would reply, "You are too young and you are not strong enough yet, George, for this hard work. You enjoy yourself while you are young. Time enough to start work when you have to."

But at the age of eight George soon found a way to start earning money, although it was not the kind of work he wanted to do. He had noticed that when gentlemen came to inspect the mine, they always had a bother to find a place to leave their horses safely. So he began to offer to hold the horses for them while they did their business. They usually gave him a copper or two in return.

One day he was holding a horse when a woman named Mrs Ainslie came up to him and said, "You seem to be very fond of animals. Would you like to look after my cows for me? I have them in a field near here, and they are always straying on to the wagon-road. Your job would be to keep them in the field. For the work I will pay you twopence a day."

George was delighted at this chance to do some real work, so he started early the next morning. He found that it was easy work, as most of the time he had only to keep his eye on the cows. So he spent his time bird's-nesting in the hedges and in making whistles from reeds and grass straws. Often a playmate, Bill Thirlwall, would come to see him, and they would then go to the brook and collect clay and make model steam-engines with it. They used many things, such as string, corks, reeds, and sticks to make their engines look realistic. All the pit-men used to admire George's skilfully made little engines. "They looked just like his father's real one," they said.

But as George grew older, Mrs Ainslie set him on to harder work, raising his wages to fourpence a day. He now had to lead the horses when they were ploughing the fields, hoe turnips, and do other farm-jobs. He soon got tired of this job and longed to be at the colliery with his father. He kept worrying his father to get him a job there, until at last Mr Stephenson came home one night and said:

"George, I have got you a job if you want it. They want a boy to drive the gin-horse, and the wages will be sixpence a day. You can start in the morning."

George knew the gin. It was a large horizontal wooden wheel which the horse pulled round and round, and so pulled up the coal from the pit by a rope. He replied:

"Thank you for getting me the job, Father, but I do not really want to drive the gin-horse. I want to help you with the engine."

"You must start at the bottom, my son," replied his father. "After you have done this job for a year or so we might get you promoted, but you can't expect to be a fireman at the start."

So George had to be content to drive the gin-horse. He did not mind the work, but all the time he longed to work on the engine. Then, when he was fourteen, the manager of the mine offered him the job of assistant fireman to his father. He was very young for such hard work and was afraid that he would not be able to keep the job. But he put all his energies into it and, when he was fifteen, succeeded well enough to get a job as fireman at another mine near by. Here he worked for two years, spending all the spare time he had in learning all about the engine he fired. It was now his ambition to become an engine-man. An engine-man looked after the works of the engine, repairing it if it went wrong, and George realized that he must understand the engine thoroughly before he could hope to take that position.

His wages were now raised to twelve shillings a week, and he felt very proud to be earning as much as a man. After two years at this work the manager of the mine where his father worked heard of George's interest in his engine, and said to him one day, "How would you like to become an engine-man, Stephenson? Do you think you could manage the work?"

This must be too good to be true, thought George. Nobody would be given such a job at his age!

Nevertheless he replied, "I have always longed to become an engine-man, sir. Give me the opportunity, and I will show you that I can do the work well."

"Well, I have decided to give you the job for a time

to see how you manage it, although you are young. Your father seems to think that you will serve me well."

So George delightedly started his new job of looking after the engine his father stoked. George loved this work. On Saturday afternoons and in other leisure hours he was usually to be found at his engine, taking it to pieces to clean it and to learn how it was constructed. He could not satisfy his thirst for knowledge about engines. His knowledge of his own engine became so good that he could always repair it himself when it went wrong. He never had to call in the colliery engineer to help, as the other enginemen did.

He still spent his spare time during the day in making clay models of all kinds of different engines he had seen or heard about. He badly wanted to make a model of some of the wonderful engines recently invented, but could find nobody who could tell him anything about them. Then one day a travelling engineer came to visit the colliery, and George asked him, "As you have travelled in many parts, perhaps you have been lucky enough to see and study the marvellous new engines. I am anxious to know how they work. Would you tell me about them?"

The engineer replied, "Yes, I have seen some, but I am in a hurry now and have no time to explain them to you. You can read all about them in books."

This baffled George. He thought to himself: "How can I learn about it from books? I have never been to school and I cannot read. The only thing to do, I suppose, is to learn to read."

So, in order to achieve his aim, he began to attend a night school at a cost of threepence a week. At the age of nineteen he was proud to be able to write his name! But he was keen to learn, and he progressed rapidly. As his reading and writing improved, he learned to do arithmetic and would study in his spare minutes by the engine fire.

In 1801, when he was twenty, George was considered such a good workman by the manager of the mine that he gave him the job of brakesman. In this job he was in charge of all the machinery which drew coal from the pit. He was also in charge of the brakes which regulated the speed of the engine and the coal-baskets as they were raised and lowered in the pit. While working at this job he first tried his skill at inventing. He was not satisfied with the way his brakes worked and spent hours trying to devise a better one, but without success.

When he was twenty-one he married and settled down in a humble cottage where, in the evenings, he would study the science of engines and in modelling experimental machines.

One day the chimney at his home caught fire. The neighbours willingly rushed in with buckets of water and threw them on the flames. They soon put the fire out, but unfortunately, in their eagerness to help, they had soaked all the furniture and left the house in terrible disorder. When George came home at night he found that a clock which hung on the wall over the fireplace had been greatly damaged with soot and water. This clock had always been one of his proudest possessions, and he. was very upset to find it in such a state.

He said to his wife in a sorrowful tone:

"Everything else can easily be cleaned and dried, but what can we do about my clock? It ought to be sent to the clock-maker's to be cleaned, but we have not enough money to pay for it."

"But, George," said his wife after a moment's thought, "could you not try to repair it yourself? You have your tools, and with a little patience you may be able to make it work again. Why do you not try?"

George's face immediately brightened up.

"I had not thought of that," he answered. "It is

worth trying. I know nothing about the works of a clock, but I can find out. I will fetch my tools and start straight away."

He was soon seated at the kitchen table taking the works to pieces. As he removed each wheel and screw, he marked their positions on a sheet of paper to make sure that he would be able to replace them correctly. Each wheel and cog he carefully cleaned free of soot and clogged oil. Then, checking every part with his drawing as he replaced it, he soon had the clock together again.

As he wound up the spring his mind was full of doubt, wondering if he had done the work properly. Would the clock go again? He gave it a shake. Sure enough, to his joy, the familiar, even *tick-tick* started. He had succeeded in his task!

The neighbours soon began to talk about George's skill as a clock-repairer and brought their clocks and watches for him to mend. He became so busy that he had to spend most of his evenings mending other people's watches. The money he received was a great help, as his wages were still low.

In 1803 a son was born to George, who named him Robert after his grandfather. George was very proud of this child, who was to grow up to become an engineer almost as famous as his father.

George continued to be the brakesman at the mine until one day the owner of a spinning-mill in Montrose, Scotland, offered him the job of looking after his steam-engine at the mill.

"Thank you kindly, sir," replied George to this offer, "but Scotland is a terrible long journey from here, and I am very happy at my job."

"That is too bad," replied the owner. "You see, we cannot get the engine to work, and I have heard that you are likely to find out what the trouble is. It is a Watt engine. If you will come I will pay you good wages."

George had already altered his mind, though, and had decided to go as soon as he heard that it was a Watt engine. Had he not been wanting to see and examine a Watt engine for years? Now here was his great opportunity.

Not being able to afford to make the journey by coach or horse, he set out for Montrose on foot. It was a long and arduous journey, but his eagerness to see the wonderful engine kept him going.

Arriving in the Scottish town, footsore and weary, he did not even wait to rest, but went straight to the spinning-mill to see the engine. It did not take him long to find out why it would not work. The pumps were continually being clogged with sand and grit which was drawn up with the water. So the next day he set to work to remedy the fault. Within a week he had invented a contrivance which prevented the sand from entering the pump, and he soon had the engine working satisfactorily.

He stayed at Montrose for twelve months, until he had a thorough knowledge of how this engine was built, and then returned to his old job of brakesman at the mine.

Later, in 1810, a new pit was sunk near the mine where he worked, and a Newcomen pumping-engine installed. George watched the engineers building this engine, and one day he said to one of them:

"This pump has not been made properly. You will never get it to work, however much you try."

The engineer merely laughed at him with scorn and said:

"Why, man, you are only a brakesman and you think you can tell us about our work? Get back to your braking, and mind you don't lose your own job through telling others theirs."

George said no more. He was content to wait and see if his ideas were right.

The pump was tried and, as George had said, failed to draw the water from the mine. The engineers tried everything to find out what was wrong, but to no avail. The owners were in despair. They could not send workmen into a flooded mine. They sent for all the engineers in the district to see if they could make the pump work, but not one could do a thing.

George just went on quietly with his own work, but on Saturday afternoons, when the engineers had left, he would go over to the engine and spend hours in examining it. He had become greatly interested in this massive piece of machinery which nobody could make work.

On one of these afternoons he was bending over the pump looking carefully at some of the working parts when he heard the voice of his foreman behind him:

"Hello, George. Studying the engine that won't work, eh? What do you make of her? Do you think you could make her go?"

George answered without hesitation:

"Why, I could alter her, man, and make her draw enough water in a week's time to send you down the mine without so much as getting your feet wet."

The foreman said no more to George, but told the manager of the mine, Mr Dodd, what George had said. Mr Dodd did not think that it was possible for George to do what engineers had failed to do, but in desperation he decided to give him a trial.

Finding George working his brakes on the next Monday morning, he said to him:

"Look here, Stephenson, I am going to give you a chance. I want you to try to repair that Newcomen engine. Set to work immediately. If you succeed where

179

other engineers have failed, depend upon it that I will make you a man for life."

George was delighted with this opportunity. He asked that he might select his own workmen. He wanted men whom he could trust to make a good job of anything he asked them to do.

So, early the next morning, he started to take the engine and pump to pieces. He made many alterations in the construction, adding new and different parts in places of many of the original ones. Within the space of three days he had the engine together again and ready for trying out. Many came to see the engine started, including the engineers who had erected it the first time and the others in the district who had tried their hands at repairing it. Everybody was anxious to see if George would be able to do as he had said.

The engine got to work slowly at first; water began to trickle from the pump-pipe. But soon, to the surprise of all the watchers, it began to spurt out in tremendous gushes. By nightfall the water in the mine was at a lower level than it had ever been before, and two days later the mine was completely dry.

George had been remarkably successful. The engineers could hardly believe their eyes as they saw the water gushing out. A common brakesman had done an engineering job which they had failed to do! It sounded incredible. George had shown the engineers how they should do their work.

Mr Dodd was so delighted that he made George a present of ten pounds and appointed him engine-man at this new pit at better wages. George's skill as an engineer soon spread round the district, and every one who had an old, rickety engine was asking him to look over it and put it right for them.

Then, in 1812, he was given another advancement in

his work. The directors of the Killingworth Colliery Company needed a new engine-wright, and Mr Dodd told them that George was the man most suitable for the work. So strong was Mr Dodd's praise for George's ability that the directors did not hesitate to appoint him. He now became in charge of all the engine-men and engines at the various mines owned by the company.

His wages were much better now than previously, but he still continued to study in the evenings. He found a friend named John Wigham, who was able to teach him to draw accurate plans of engines. This knowledge helped him greatly in his work. Also, he still carried on his experiments with new kinds of engines and machines and spent many hours making his models of these. His son, Robert, had now grown into a bright lad and often helped his father with these models. Father and son spent many evenings together, both finding great enjoyment in the work.

When Robert was twelve his father decided to send him to school so that he might learn to read and write. He decided upon an expensive school in Newcastle to send Robert to, but his wife, when he told her, said:

"It will cost us far more than we can afford to send Robert to such a smart school. You will never find the money to pay the fees."

But George replied:

"I am anxious that Robert should have a greater opportunity to learn to read and write than I did as a boy, and the only chance for him to get it is to send him to a good school. I can soon earn enough money to pay for it by repairing clocks and watches again in the evenings as I did years ago."

So Robert started school, and his father again took in watches and clocks to repair.

At about this time the coal-trade was expanding so

rapidly that to take the coal over the country in horse-drawn wagons was becoming too slow a method of transport. The mine-owners could not deliver their orders quickly enough to satisfy their customers. People were beginning to talk of the possibility of using steam-engines on wheels to draw the wagons along, but not much progress in inventing anything useful had as yet taken place.

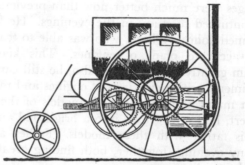

TREVITHICK'S STEAM-CARRIAGE

It is true that, nearly fifty years before, a French engineer had built a steam-wagon which ran fairly well, but it was never put to any use. William Murdock constructed a model of one of these engines in Cornwall in the year 1784, but owing to some trouble he abandoned it.

Then Richard Trevithick patented an invention for an engine which he called a 'steam-carriage' in 1802. This engine, when completed, created great interest. Trevithick took it to London to show it to the great scientists. They were extremely pleased with its performance, but later Trevithick abandoned this engine because the roads were in too bad a state for it to run on.

A year later he built another one. This was successful enough to be able to pull a number of wagons along cast-iron rails at a speed of five miles an hour. Unfortunately, though, the weight of the engine kept smashing up the rails, and so it was never used to any purpose.

A colliery-owner, named Blackett, of Wylam—George Stephenson's birthplace—had seen Trevithick's first engine in London and, being convinced that it could be made to work, started experiments in building a better one. He employed an engineer named John Steele to build it, but the engine turned out to be a failure.

But Mr Blackett continued to spend time and money on his experiments, and at last he got an engine built which just managed to crawl along at a speed of five miles in six hours !

George Stephenson had also begun to study and experiment with models of steam-carriages at Killingworth colliery. Now that he was the engine-wright he was responsible for the cartage of the coal, and he was continually trying to find a means of doing it at less cost.

He had heard of the attempts of others to build locomotives and saw that great things might come of a good travelling engine which was capable of hauling trucks of coal. So, to know how far the other inventors had progressed in their ideas, he obtained plans of all the travelling engines that had ever been built. George found all these engines expensive to make and costly to run, and he felt sure that he could build a better one. He made a number of journeys over to Wylam to study the works of Mr Blackett's locomotive.

Then he set about making plans for his own. He sorted out all the best ideas from the other engines and used them in his design. Eventually he had his plans complete to start building, but now he needed money for materials and to pay workmen. He was in a dilemma about it until Mr Dodd suggested that he ask Lord Ravensworth, the owner of the mine where he worked, to lend him a sufficient sum.

183

So when he next saw Lord Ravensworth, George went up to him and said:

"My lord, I wish to ask of you a very great favour. I want to build a steam-engine to run on wheels. I have worked out my idea, but I have no money to carry it out with. As I think my engine will be very useful at the mine I am being bold enough to ask you to pay for building it. I have great faith in this engine and I promise you that you will not regret it, my lord."

Lord Ravensworth considered it for a while and then asked, "How fast do you think it will run? Are you sure it will not turn out a failure?"

George replied, "I am certain that I can make it work, my lord, and there is no limit to the speed it might go if the works can be made well enough to stand the strain."

So Lord Ravensworth decided to pay for the cost of building the engine, and George went away to make arrangements to start the work. But he soon found many unexpected difficulties came in the way. He could not find workmen skilled enough to do the accurate work necessary, and found that before a start could be made he must instruct and train them into doing the work as he required it. Then the tools available at the mines were of poor quality, and special ones had to be made.

But in July, 1814, after much labour, anxiety, and frequent alterations, Stephenson's first locomotive was ready to be tested. It worked far better than any previous engine, George found, but he was far from satisfied with it. After a few trials he saw many defects in the mechanism and design and decided to build a second and better one.

As his engine was to be far better than any before, he took out a patent for it so that nobody could steal his ideas. This time Mr Dodd provided the necessary money for the work.

The engine was finished in the summer of 1815 and
proved to be so successful that it was put into regular
service at the mine to haul the coal-wagons.

At about this time George was also very concerned
about the numbers of miners who were continually being

MODEL OF STEPHENSON'S SECOND LOCOMOTIVE, 1815
From a model in the Science Museum, South Kensington, London

killed through explosions of gas in the mine. After one of
these tragedies he stood at the pit-head thoughtfully,
wondering how the explosions could be avoided, when a
bystander turned angrily to him and said:

"You are the engine-wright at this place. Why don't
you do something about it instead of standing there while
the miners get killed?"

This woke George from his reverie. Banging his fists
together, he cried:

"By Heavens, I will, too! It sickens me to see so many
men killed through no fault of their own."

185

So, having made up his mind, he went home and began to puzzle out how he could prevent these explosions. He knew that they were caused by the flames from the miners' candles lighting the foul gas. But the miners had to have lights to see to do their work. Thinking in this way, he began to see the need for some kind of lamp the miners could carry which would not ignite the gas. So he set to work to invent one.

He spent many hours working out an idea, and then got a lamp which he had designed made at the local blacksmith's.

When Mr Dodd saw it he said to George:

"The idea looks all right, George, but we must have it tested to make sure. It might not work properly. I will send a miner down the pit to see if there is any risk of an explosion with it."

"No, you cannot do that, Mr Dodd," replied George promptly. "Why should a miner risk his life with my invention? I will go down myself to test it. Then if anything is wrong with it, I shall deserve to be blown up for having invented it. But I am not afraid. I have faith in my lamp."

So on the next night George was lowered into the pit with his lighted safety-lamp. He carried it to the most dangerous passage in the mine and blocked it up with boards so that the foul gas would be allowed to accumulate. Nervously he waited and watched. At first the flame burned steadily; then, as the gas filled the air, it began to flicker, and finally went out. George was delighted. The lamp was a success. No more miners need lose their lives through explosions!

So although Sir Humphry Davy is always known as the inventor of the first safety-lamp, the credit is really due to George Stephenson, who made and tested his lamp months before Davy got the idea.

The safety-lamp finished, George turned his mind back to his locomotives. He was still not satisfied with his work. He knew he could build a better engine.

Then another colliery company at Hetton saw how successful his railway was working at Killingsworth and asked him to build a similar one for them. On the day

HETTON COLLIERY
From a lithograph in the Science Museum, South Kensington, London

of the opening of this railway, crowds of people watched this new miracle engine draw seventeen wagons, loaded with coal, at a speed of four miles an hour!

Other orders for colliery railways followed and kept George busy. But he was not satisfied. He wanted to do something bigger than a colliery railway.

Then his chance came. In the year 1821 he heard that a company were considering building a long railway from Stockton to Darlington, so he went to see Mr Pease, the manager, about it.

"If you have not yet appointed an engineer for your proposed railway, may I offer myself for the job?" he asked Mr Pease. "I am the engine-wright at Killingsworth Colliery, and I have had some experience in building locomotives."

"Why do you want to leave your present work and come to us?" asked Mr Pease.

"I want to increase my experience of building railways." replied George, "and this one seems to offer me that opportunity."

"I see. But how do I know that you are capable of the work? I have only your word for it," went on Mr Pease.

"You have only to come to Killingsworth to see my engines at work, sir, for seeing is believing."

So Mr Pease made the journey to George's mine. He was delighted with what he saw, so George got the job.

His son, Robert, who had recently left college, went to help him with the work. Together they planned out the route the line was to take and then supervised the building of the locomotives and wagons.

The railway was opened, with great ceremony, on a day in September, 1825. Vast crowds of people came to see these new locomotives start. They had never seen a railway before. Many expected to see the great hissing boilers of the engines burst under the pressure of the steam. But everything went off as planned. George drove the engine, which was coupled to six wagons of coal and twenty wagons fitted with seats for passengers. All the way from Stockton to Darlington the onlookers cheered and shouted as the engine passed them.

A newspaper reporter wrote in his paper the next day:

The signal being given, the engine started off with this immense train of carriages; and such was its power that in some parts it reached the stupendous speed of twelve miles an hour! There were about six hundred people packed in or hanging on the sides of the wagons. Great excitement abounded everywhere.

After this success George, with Mr Pease as partner, built a factory at Newcastle to make locomotives in large numbers. He fully expected that railways would be wanted all over England as soon as people saw those he had already constructed. But unfortunately this was not so. for many did not trust this new-fangled invention.

STEPHENSON'S No. 1 ENGINE AT DARLINGTON

They preferred to keep using the old methods of transport. George went about doing his utmost to convince the public of the advantages of his locomotives. He would say:

"Before many years have passed you will find that locomotive railways will be the great highways of the world."

But few believed him. Even well-known engineers laughed at his wild sayings. Consequently his business began to suffer, as no orders came in.

Then George was appointed engineer for a railway to be built from Liverpool to Manchester. At first, however, this did nothing to help his factory, because the company who were building the railway had not decided what form of transport to use.

Even when the route was laid out with lines ready for opening, they had come to no decision. George did his utmost to persuade them to use locomotives, but other engineers were also busy persuading them to use other methods.

Eventually the company suggested that Mr Stephenson should build one of his locomotives and test it on their lines. This he did, but still, although it worked well, no decision was reached as to what should be used permanently.

Finally, after much persuasion from George Stephenson, the company decided to offer a prize of five hundred pounds to the engineer who made and delivered the best locomotive on their railway. The date fixed for the contest was October 1, 1829.

Here was George's chance to show the world how great his engine really was! With Robert to help him, he set to work to prepare plans for his new locomotive. Then the work of building it was started at his Newcastle works. George took pains to see that only the best of materials and workmanship were put into this new engine. He was anxious to carry off that prize!

When the locomotive was finished, Mr Stephenson named it the *Rocket* and had it sent to Liverpool ready for the great day.

Other engineers all over the country had been trying to build engines for the competition, but only three succeeded in finishing them.

On the day, engineers and scientists arrived at Liverpool from all parts to see the display. Many thousands of spectators lined the route the engines were to take. A grand-stand was built to accommodate well-known people, and streamers were flying everywhere.

Each locomotive in turn had to be driven backward

and forward over a two-mile stretch until it had completed a journey of seventy miles. The *Rocket* did the journey without trouble at an average speed of fifteen miles an hour.

After the judges had counted up the points they had

"ROCKET' LOCOMOTIVE, 1829
From the original in the Science Museum, South Kensington, London

awarded to each entry in the competition, they declared, amid great enthusiasm, that the *Rocket* was by far the best locomotive there and that it had won the prize.

George and his son were delighted. Praise was showered upon them from all quarters. George was satisfied because he had proved to the world that locomotives were unequalled for transporting goods over long distances.

191

From the day of the success of the *Rocket*, Stephenson's firm became very busy. Orders for the construction of locomotive railways continually poured in. Railway tracks began to spring up all over England. And so this building of railways has been going on ever since, to make the elaborate system of railways that we have in England to-day.

At the age of sixty George Stephenson retired from his great work of engineering and left his business in charge of his son, Robert, who by this time had become almost as famous for his engineering as his father.

Seven years later, on the twelfth of August, 1848, George Stephenson died, a happy man, having satisfied his great ambition of seeing locomotive railways being used over the length and breadth of England.

XI

WILLIAM MORRIS

Artist-craftsman

ON March 24, 1834, just over one hundred years ago, a baby boy was born at a large house in Walthamstow, near London.

WILLIAM MORRIS
From a painting by G. F. Watts. National Portrait Gallery

When his father, Mr Morris, gave him the name of William, he little thought that in later years this name would become famous all over the world.

It was fortunate for William that his parents were fairly wealthy, because in those days a child born to poor parents lived a very miserable and unhappy life. The reason was this. For the previous hundred years machines had been used for making things which had formerly been made by hand by the craftsmen in their homes. Cotton and woollen goods were no longer woven by

193

mothers and fathers on their little hand-looms in their kitchens. The coming of the machines had stopped all that. Looms were large and expensive to buy, and needed steam-engines to work them. The poor workers could not afford to buy them, so wealthy men built large factories, filled them with these machines, and persuaded the people to leave their homes to go and work for them.

This should have made the lives of the workers happier and more comfortable, because machines make work easier and articles cheaper. But instead, the masters were cruel and wanted large profits for themselves, so they made the workers toil long hours each day for very small wages. Men would only earn about eight shillings a week. Women and small children also were made to work from early morning to late at night.

Can you imagine children of nine years working for thirteen hours a day in the coal-mines hauling heavy trucks of coal? Then, when the day's toil was over, they would go home, in ragged clothes, tired out and sore-footed, to a dirty hovel to sleep for a few hours until it was time to start work again at daybreak? This is how the poor children of those days lived.

William Morris, in his early years, knew nothing of these cruelties going on round him. He was always blessed with plenty of good food, warm clothes, and a comfortable bed in which to sleep. His father had an office in London, to which he journeyed each day by coach. On Sundays the whole family used to attend church regularly, and during the week William was taught by a governess to read and write.

William was keen on reading, and by the time he was four he had already read many of Sir Walter Scott's novels. Strangely enough, though, it was years before he could write, and he never could spell words well.

WILLIAM MORRIS

When William was six the family moved to a house on the edge of Epping Forest called Woodford Hall. The forest became a fine playground for William. Whenever he was free from lessons he would wander into the forest to spend an enchanting hour among the birds and trees. Everything there seemed so peaceful and beautiful. He learned to use a gun to shoot the animals and birds, but one day a friend, on being proudly shown a rabbit William had shot, said, "William, it is cruel to shoot harmless animals. You should take a book and pencil into the forest and learn to make drawings of them. Then you will stop wanting to kill them."

William took this advice, and soon found his friend's words to be correct. He found it far more fun sitting quietly writing and watching until a rabbit came and squatted in an opening so that he could make a sketch of it.

At the age of nine he was sent to a preparatory school to improve his education. Here he found great pleasure in making things with his hands and in continuing his sketching. After five years at this school his father transferred him to the famous Marlborough College. By this time William had grown into a thick-set, sturdy boy with red cheeks and black curly hair. He had also developed a violent temper which stood him in good stead at this school, for in those days the older boys at boarding-schools were great bullies. William soon found this out, for on his second day there a group of older boys called across the school quadrangle to him, "Hi! You! Come here, boy. We want you. What is your name?"

William looked at them with a frown; being a new-comer, however, he thought it best not to offend them, and answered:

"Morris. What do you want with me?"

"You will see soon enough. You're a new boy, aren't

you? Then it is time you were conducted round the school," said one in reply, with a sly smile on his lips.

William had no time to tell them that he would prefer to find his way about alone, for they had grabbed him and were marching him towards the building. Two other new boys were treated similarly, and the procession entered the building. Through the corridors and up the stairs they went, and eventually stopped outside the dormitory.

Then one of the captors shouted, "We want a sheet. Fetch a sheet, somebody."

The sheet was fetched and laid out on the landing-floor. William stood by with a puzzled look on his face as one of the other new boys was lifted off his feet and laid clumsily on the sheet. Four of the biggest boys then lifted the sheet by the corners and, to William's horror, swung it over the stair banisters so that it hung suspended high above the floor below. The boy in the sheet had turned white with terror, but the group of bullies, thinking it great fun, were roaring with laughter.

William, realizing that his turn to suffer this bullying was to come, became violently angry. Bursting free from his astonished captors, he flew at the others and shouted:

"Pull that sheet back, you great bullies."

The bullies burst out laughing and jeering until, most unexpectedly, William's fist shot out. Bang! Down went one boy like a ninepin. The others, startled at this sudden attack from one so young, pulled the sheet back on to the landing and made a rush for William, crying, "We will give you something for that. We'll teach you to have more respect for your elders."

But William did not care. He was livid with rage. Round and round went his arms like windmill sails, striking out at anyone who came near him. Then, together, they made a rush at him, bowling him over. Quickly two boys jumped on him, pinning his arms to the floor. But before they could hurt him some one shouted "*Cave.*" That meant that a master was in sight. Immediately there was a rush and scramble to get away, and in less than a minute William, breathless and dishevelled, found himself alone. He had been saved from the bullies!

After this experience the older boys had more respect for William's strength and temper and never attempted to bully him again. Nevertheless, they thought him a queer sort of fellow. He would not join in games. He was not interested in cricket and football. He much preferred to spend his leisure hours in reading or sketching or walking in Savernake Forest near by, to watch the birds and animals. He collected birds' eggs, but was always careful never to upset the nest or take more than one egg from it. He also became very interested in art and spent many hours in the school library reading books about it.

But he could not live happily without using his hands. He was always wanting to make something. There was not much opportunity for hobbies at this school, and the only one he could find to do was to make nets.

For hours he would sit in the common-room with his net strung between two chairs, knotting and joining the strands of tarred twine together. He was oblivious to the noise and hubbub of the other boys round him, and they took no notice of him. They had become accustomed to his queer ways by now.

During one of his holidays his father asked him what he would like to become when he grew up.

"I would like to be a craftsman, father," he replied promptly, "so that I may make beautiful things. The horribly ugly things made these days by machines make me want to show the people craftwork which is beautiful as well as fit to use. Our lives would be much happier if we filled our homes with beautiful furniture, carpets, and curtains."

"William!" ejaculated his astonished father. "Do you realize what you are saying? You are the son of a gentleman, and only the poor work with their hands. Here you have anything that money can buy, and you ask to be nothing more than a common labourer. You must learn a profession which is worthy of your position. You can become a soldier, sailor, or clergyman, but never a labourer. So please do not mention such a ridiculous career to me again."

William, realizing that it was useless trying to show his father how he yearned to work with his hands, gave in and agreed to become a clergyman. So he returned to school, deciding to work hard to become a preacher as his father wished. But during his last term at school in 1851, another incident happened which renewed his old yearnings to become a craftsman.

A great exhibition of craftwork was being held in Hyde Park. The lately famous Crystal Palace was erected there to house it. At the time this great building, composed entirely of glass and steel girders, was considered a wonderful feat of engineering. Everybody who could afford it wanted to go and see it.

William's parents took him there on the opening day, but on passing through the turnstiles, William glanced round, and a look of disgust came over his face. He was shocked with the rows and rows of ugly machines, furniture, pottery, and textiles which met his gaze.

Turning to his father, he exclaimed, "How wonderfully ugly it all is! It is too terrible for words. I will not walk round to see all this ugly stuff."

"You must come round," commanded his mother sharply. "We have made this special journey to show you this wonderful exhibition. All the finest things that can be made are here for us to see. Do not act in such a silly manner. Come along at once, or I shall get cross with you."

Thereupon William flew into a violent rage and, bouncing down into a near-by seat, shouted, "I tell you I will not go one step farther. Wild horses will not drag me round."

After further remonstrances the parents found it impossible to make William change his mind, so they left him in the seat while they went off alone.

This experience reawakened William's desire to become a craftsman, but he dared not mention it to his parents again. He had agreed to become a clergyman, and it was for him to forget his desires. His mother and father would never agree to any other career for him now.

William did not remain at Marlborough many weeks after the visit to the exhibition. This was due to a riot at the school. The boys had suddenly revolted against the headmaster, and they barricaded him in his room. For some days the school was in a state of great confusion, and the news of the riot filled the newspapers. Mr Morris read about it and was so disgusted that his son should attend such a wild and unruly school that he took him away and hired a private tutor to teach him at home.

Two years later, at the age of nineteen, William went to Exeter College, Oxford, to receive his final training for becoming a clergyman. He made friends with another student named Edward Burne-Jones. They sat next to each other at meals and soon found that they enjoyed each other's company. Edward was studying to become an artist, and as William was also keen on art they found much to talk about. Morris had found some one who would listen to him without sneering when he talked about his hatred of machines and the ugliness of the articles made on them. They also discussed the distressing state in which the poor people lived, and wondered how they could set about doing something for them.

Eventually they formed a group of friends who all had the same kind of ideas.

This group they called 'the Order of Sir Galahad,' and they pledged themselves to work to make the lives of the slum-dwellers better and happier. Morris was appointed the leader. His friends thought him a very clever fellow, but his tutor at college wrote on his report, "He has no special literary tastes or capacity." Little did he know about his student when he wrote that, for at that time William was engaged in his spare time writing a clever poem, the first of many which were to make his name famous throughout the world.

One night, in September, 1854, the friends were gathered together in William's room when he brought out a bundle of papers and announced:

"I have here a long poem which I have composed. Will one of you read it aloud, and then you others can tell me what you think of it?"

Burne-Jones took the papers and began to read. The friends listened intently, nodding their heads with approval as the beautiful lines and phrases struck their ears. When the reading ended, the fellows surrounded William and cried, calling him by his nickname:

"Good old Topsy! It is marvellous! Behold, before us stands a famous poet of the future. We did not know you had it in you to write such beautiful stuff, Topsy."

They were joking over his becoming a famous poet—but how true it was to be!

Morris so hated machinery for all the evil its use had brought into the lives of the people that when he went on his first holiday to France with Burne-Jones, he walked everywhere, sometimes making his feet sore and blistered, rather than use a train.

Burne-Jones told him not to be so silly, but he replied:

"I hate the nasty brimstone, noisy, shrieking railway

train that cares not twopence for hill or valley, poplar-tree or lime-tree, corn-poppy or blue cornflower. I would rather blister my feet a hundred times than ride in a train."

One night the two friends were walking along the quay at Le Havre, talking about the work they would do when they left college. Topsy said, "I promised my parents that I would become a clergyman, but I do not want to. I am sure I could do much more good in some other work. I am not quite sure, though, what I want to do."

"Well, I have made up my mind to become an artist," replied Burne-Jones. "In that way I might give to the world more beauty through my pictures. Why do you not become an architect and build better houses for people to live in? You could do a lot of good by refusing to build hovels and showing the landlords that every person should have a house fit to live in."

"That is a good idea," replied Topsy after some thought. "If I could do something to help the miserable workers in the factories I should be happy."

So it was decided, and back at college, William worked hard for his degree, ready to start on his career as an architect. In his spare time he continued writing poems and had changed his earlier hobby of netting to engraving pictures on wood.

By this time William had become very wealthy, as his father had died and left him a fortune. He could easily have lived the life of a gentleman without working if he had so wished; but the urge to help the poor was too strong in him.

After leaving college William, much to his mother's despair, went to work for an architect named Street at Oxford. In this office he became very friendly with another young architect named Philip Webb. They spent most of their spare time together walking about the country, studying the architecture of churches and other buildings. Webb had already worked at Wolverhampton and Reading, and he knew much about the slum-dwellings in these towns. Telling William about the awful lives the poor people lived, Webb made him more anxious to do something to relieve their misery.

Towards the end of his first year's work Mr Street moved his office to London. Here William went to live in rooms in Bloomsbury with his friend, Ted Burne-Jones. Ted had been in London for a year studying painting.

One evening a friend of Ted's, a well-known artist named Rossetti, came to see them. After some general talk the conversation led to painting and art, and Rossetti said to William:

"You should start painting. You would make a good artist. I will give you all the help I can."

"Yes, why not try your hand, Topsy?" put in Ted. "It will be grand fun painting together."

So Morris started painting in his spare time. Rossetti often came in to give the friends advice, and after a time William began to do some excellent work.

This year of 1856 was a very busy one for William, for besides his work at the office and his painting, he wrote much poetry for the *Oxford and Cambridge Magazine*. Towards the end of the year he again upset his mother by telling her that he had decided to give up architecture for painting.

"Will you ever know what you want to do?" she asked. "First you are going to be a clergyman, then an architect, and now a painter! It is a great pity that I allowed you to change your mind the first time. What is the use of trying to paint? No one will want to buy your paintings. You are just wasting your time."

But William had decided. He gave up the office-work and spent his days with Ted, composing poetry and painting. He used to frighten Ted sometimes with his tempers. If his work went wrong he would get excited, jump and dance, and throw books and chairs about the room. Once he kicked a panel out of the door in his rage. He could never work quietly.

During the next year the two painters moved into larger rooms in Red Lion Square, London. The furniture in these rooms was so ugly and uncomfortable that, on seeing it, William flew into a rage.

"Look at the horrible stuff," he raved. "The chairs are smothered with ugly twists and curves which people think beautiful, although they give you a pain in the back to sit in them, I'll be bound. What is the use of a chair if it is uncomfortable? If you don't make chairs to sit in, why not make saucepans without bottoms? Both things are just as silly."

When his anger had abated, he set about designing his own furniture, making sure that it would be useful, comfortable, and also of good appearance. He gave an order to a local carpenter to make the furniture from his designs, and when it was finished he took all the old stuff into the back yard and made a bonfire of it.

The two painters were now beginning to obtain a few orders for their work. The first big piece of work they were asked to do was to decorate the walls of the debating rooms at Oxford University. Rossetti and Philip Webb went to Oxford with them to help.

The paintings were to be of historical scenes—one to cover each panel of the walls. In order to do the work as accurately as possible Morris designed and had models made of various things they were to include in the paintings so that they could copy them. For instance, a suit of armour was made by a local blacksmith and set up in the hall, so that the artists could copy it when they were painting the knights in the pictures.

For some time Morris had also been experimenting in other crafts. He still had the urge to do good craftwork He was learning to carve in wood and stone. He had been picking old tapestries to pieces, thread by thread, to

THE BIRD: WOOLLEN TEXTILE DESIGNED AND WOVEN BY
WILLIAM MORRIS
Victoria and Albert Museum

see how they were made. When he had found out how the skilful makers of these tapestries had worked, he set about weaving one, containing a beautiful pattern of birds and trees.

He was still writing poems, too, and his first book, called *The Defence of Guenevere*, was published in March, 1858. Only two hundred copies of this book were sold, but he was beginning to become known as a poet.

In the summer of the same year he went for a holiday to France with Philip Webb.

Previously he had met a young lady whom he wished to marry, and he said to Philip as they crossed to France:

"Philip, I am going to be married, and I want a house built. Will you design it for me? But I warn you, it has got to be a very special house. I want to show these shoddy builders how to build solidly and well. Two things I ask: that it be fit to live in and good to look at."

The two friends spent most of their holiday drawing up the plans for the house. The pages of the guide-book they took with them were covered with pencil sketches of ideas they had thought out.

On returning home, Webb set to work to draw the proper plans for the builders, while Morris spent much time designing the furniture.

When everything was ready to start building, Morris gathered his friends together and suggested that they should all help in building and decorating the house.

The walls were built with bright red bricks, so it was given the name of 'Red House.'

Philip Webb guided the builders, Rossetti and Burne-Jones led the artists in decorating the walls of the rooms, and Morris painted flower-patterns on some of the walls so that it resembled wallpaper. Morris was also supervising the carpenters, who were making the furniture to his design. His wife—he had already married—started embroidering curtains and cloths. She was a newcomer to the circle of friends, but she soon fell in with their industrious habits.

Not even the glass for the windows was of good enough quality to satisfy Morris, so Webb designed that, and had it specially made. Everything that was put into the house had to be of excellent design and workmanship.

In 1860 the house was finished, and William took his wife there to live. The friends who had helped in the building came down at the week-ends to admire their work and have interesting talks on art and crafts.

Then, during one of these talks, Morris had an idea. He said, "Between us we have accomplished a great work. We have built a house that is worthy of its name. But need that be the last of our work together? Why should we not join together and work to make beautiful and useful craftwork for one another's homes?"

"How do you propose to do this?" queried one of them. "It will not be easy to work together if we can only meet at the week-ends."

"My idea is that you should all give up your present work, and then we can start a business as craftworkers. We can each pursue our own crafts and so help one another to fill our homes with good things," replied Morris.

"But we cannot start a business without money, and we cannot run it without profits. We must earn something to live," said Burne-Jones doubtfully.

"That need not worry you. I have ample money with which to start, and we might sell an occasional piece of work to help us along. Anyway, we can at least try the experiment," replied William eagerly.

The others began to catch some of William's enthusiasm for the idea, and it was eventually agreed to set up the business as soon as possible.

A workshop was obtained in London, and the firm was named Morris, Marshall, Faulkner, & Co., fine-art workmen in painting, carving, furniture, and metals. All the friends, including Morris, Burne-Jones, Rossetti, Faulkner, Marshall, Brown, and Webb, were partners in the venture. A few men and boys were employed to carry out the smaller jobs, and women to embroider cloths and curtains.

Greatly to their surprise, their excellent work soon attracted much attention, and they began to receive numerous orders for work.

In 1862 another great exhibition of craftwork was held in London, and when Morris heard about it he called the others together and said:

"Let us have a stand in this exhibition so that we may display our work to all. Even if we do not sell anything, it will serve to show people the real ugliness of the work of other manufacturers. In that way we might do some good."

So work was prepared and sent to the exhibition, and Morris & Co. won the two gold medals given for the finest craftwork on show. All the visitors were loud in their praises for Morris's clever craftsmanship, much to the disgust of the other manufacturers. Some of these were so jealous that they tried to get Morris disqualified by telling the exhibition committee that his stained glass was really old glass taken out of church windows and had not been made by the firm of Morris & Co. at all.

"Morris & Co. are frauds," they said. "We demand that they lose their gold medals and that these be awarded to some other craftsman."

The committee considered their complaint but replied that the glass had been designed and made by the workers of Morris & Co. This success for Morris spread like wildfire, and orders came pouring in. The greedy manufacturers, instead of harming Morris's business as they had intended, had helped it!

Soon after this Morris began designing beautiful wallpapers. Such appalling wallpapers were being sold all over the country that Morris thought it his duty to teach the people to appreciate and buy better ones to make their homes beautiful. Morris's papers soon became famous for their beautiful patterns and colours.

The firm continued to prosper, and it became necessary to move into larger premises. But for all that, the business was not making any profits, for Morris could not be persuaded to charge enough money for the work. Often craftwork was sold for less than it cost to make, so that anybody who appreciated it could have it for what they could afford to pay. Morris always felt that it was wrong to deny people beautiful things because they had not the money to buy them.

He still continued to write and publish his poems. He often composed them as he stood at his easel designing a wallpaper or painting a frieze.

The largest piece of work the firm had to do came to them in 1867, when they were asked to decorate the walls of a large room in the Victoria and Albert Museum in London. They employed a number of extra artists for this work, each to paint one panel of the walls.

Morris did not see the work until it was complete. When he did he scrutinized each panel carefully, and as he passed along the walls his anger began to rise. The work was not up to his standard. He had noticed faults in it. Burne-Jones, who accompanied him, noticed his mood but could not understand the reason. The paintings looked excellent to him. But he had not long to wonder, for Morris suddenly burst out angrily with the words:

"This work is no good. The panels do not match one another. Those fools of painters have varied their designs. We cannot leave it like this. It will all have to be done again."

"Do not be silly," replied Burne-Jones after he had recovered from his surprise. It was too small a fault to bother about. "It will cost us far more than we can afford to have all this repainted. After all, all the panels are excellently painted, so what does it matter if they are not quite like one another? Nobody will notice it."

"What does it matter, indeed?" stormed Morris, stamping his feet in rage. "Can we, as craftsmen, allow such mistakes to pass by? That is how the shoddy manu- facturers do their work. It is going to be repainted, and I will take care to see that it is done right this time. I will have one painter do all the panels, and I will see that he makes no mistakes. It is appalling."

Morris, true to his word, found a painter named Fair- fax Murray and ordered him to repaint the whole of the room. Morris would not pass any work which was not perfect.

At about this time Morris published his greatest poem, called *Jason*. This book made him famous. It was a brilliant piece of work, and Morris received praise from far and wide.

Each year Morris found new crafts with which to experiment. In 1870 he was to be found spending much time illuminating the borders of pages in books.

Then, in 1871, tired of living among the ugliness of London's streets—he had moved from the Red House some time previously to be nearer his workshop—he bought a house in the country called Kelmscott Manor. His old friend Rossetti went to live with him.

But even here he could not escape from his passion for improving things. One day he went into the market town near to his new house and saw workmen repairing the church. He quickly noticed that they were making an ugly job of it and went to see the vicar, hoping that he might make the workmen alter and improve their work.

Finding the vicar at home, he said to him:

"What a horrible mess those builders are making of

your church! They will completely spoil its beauty. Go and stop them before it is too late."

The vicar, taken aback at his rudeness, replied crossly, "I ordered them to do the work, and I can do what I please. Who are you to interfere with my business? Why, if I want to stand on my head in the aisle of my church nobody is going to stop me. It would be well if you minded your own business, sir. Good day."

Morris went away determined to do something about it. There were so many churches being spoilt through careless restoration. So in 1877 he started a Society for the Protection of Ancient Buildings. Many well-known people joined it, including John Ruskin and Thomas Carlyle. By means of lectures and pamphlets they tried to teach the public how to repair these buildings properly.

Some good came of Morris's work in this direction, but not nearly so much as he had hoped.

The firm of Morris was now becoming so famous for its beautifully designed wallpapers, stained glass, embroidery, painted tiles, and furniture that other manufacturers were beginning to copy them. They found that their shoddy stuff would not sell so easily now that Morris's could be bought at reasonable prices. But this is just what Morris wanted to happen. He did not mind their stealing his ideas and designs. Had he not been working all his life to try to get people to make and buy more beautiful things?

By the year 1876 William Morris was a name familiar to people all over the country. Various societies were clamouring for him to lecture to them on art and crafts. The standard of craftsmanship throughout the country was gradually improving under his influence.

As he got older, he left most of the business-work to his manager and spent his time working at various crafts just for the pleasure of it. After so many years of toil

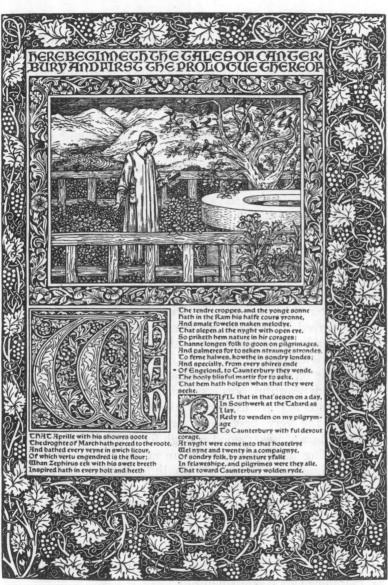

A Page (reduced) from "The Works of Geoffrey Chaucer," printed by William Morris at the Kelmscott Press, Hammersmith, 1896

Victoria and Albert Museum

with his hands he could not give it up now. He built a loom in his house and began weaving carpets, which soon became popular, as did any other work he attempted.

Although he had achieved the highest success in many different crafts, there was still one craft that he had for long wanted to excel in. That was the craft of printing. He longed to make beautiful books, but he had never found the time to learn how to print and bind them.

Then, when he was fifty-six years old, he went one day to a lecture on printing given by a friend named Emery Walker. So impressed was he with it that he said to Walker afterwards:

"Your lecture has renewed my desire to learn to print good books. I wonder if you would help me to make a new fount of type—one that excels any for beauty and cleverness? Let us give to the world better books, worthy of the printer's craft."

Walker was pleased at his friend's interest in printing and agreed to become his partner in the work. They started a business which they called the Kelmscott Press.

Morris learned the art of making and casting type-letters. Then he set to work to design a fount of letters. He also designed beautiful borders and headings for the pages. He wrote to various people all over Europe trying to obtain the very best paper and inks. Second best of anything was never good enough for William Morris.

Printing his first book was an exciting task. As each succeeding page came off his little hand-press, so he enjoyed his work more.

Then in January, 1891, his first book appeared on the market, beautifully printed and bound. It was called *The Story of the Glittering Plain.*

Everybody was delighted with this book and, as with any work Morris ever did, they judged it to be a wonderful example of good craftsmanship.

Sixty-two books in all were produced at the Kelmscott Press, and there is no doubt that much of the improvement in modern book-production is due to the great work of Morris.

William Morris died on October 3, 1896, at the age of sixty-two, but the spirit and influence of his great work as an artist-craftsman is as much alive to-day as it was during the latter years of his life.

WILLIAM MORRIS

XII
THOMAS ALVA EDISON
Electrical Engineer

IT was a summer's day in the year 1854. The expanse of Lake Huron could be seen from the shore, brightly spotted

THOMAS ALVA EDISON
Photo: E. Bieber

with gaily coloured steamboats, tall-masted sailing-ships, and every style of craft imaginable. At one point on the edge of the vast lake stood a tall wooden tower. Gazing at the tower was a small crowd of people who had just alighted from a pleasure-steamer. They were waiting their turns for the telescope on the high platform at the top of the tower so as to look at the miles of wonderful wooded country round.

This tower had been an idea of a villager of Port Huron named Samuel Edison. He had built the tower and now charged visitors twenty-five cents for the novelty of seeing so many miles of beautiful country at a glance. He did good business in the holiday season, but nobody enjoyed the sensation of sitting perched on its high platform, telescope raised to his eye, more than his seven-year-old son Thomas Alva, known to his playmates and family as young Al.

Al was a very inquisitive child by nature. He was always experimenting to find out things for himself. At the age of four it is said that he tried to hatch some ducks' eggs by sitting on them, for he thought that if the ducks could do it so could he. At another time he set fire to his father's barn to see how quickly it would burn. He must have had many good spankings for his childish tricks!

Whenever there were visitors at the tower Al was not allowed to use it. At these times he would spend hours in the cellar at home experimenting. On shelves round the walls he kept a large collection of bottles and jars filled with various chemicals. His mother and father were rather nervous about one so young using these chemicals, and one day his mother, seeing one of Al's playmates taste something from one of the bottles, became angry and cried:

"Al, you will be poisoning somebody one of these days. I will not let you keep these dangerous chemicals any longer. Throw them all away at once, and give up your silly games."

"Oh, Mother," cried Al, bursting into tears, "do let me keep them. I have such fun playing with them. I promise I won't let anybody else touch them, if only you'll let me keep them."

"Well, perhaps you may, if you keep your promise," replied his mother, after some hesitation. "But you must keep them locked up in future when you are not using them. They are not safe left lying about for anyone to pick up."

Thus Al was provided with a cupboard with a lock so that he could continue his experiments with safety.

215

When he was nine his mother bought him a book about chemistry, and from it he learnt to do many new experiments.

For a time he attended the village school, but one day he went running home, sobbing heartily. His mother asked him what was the matter, and he replied between sobs:

"I heard my teacher tell the inspector that I am addled and not clever enough to be kept at school. They think I am a dunce, and all the boys are making fun of me."

"Oh, so that is the trouble," answered his mother, angry at the teacher for having said that her child was dull. "But never mind, Al, you need not go to school again. I will teach you your lessons myself, and we will show them that you are not such a dunce."

Al was so grateful to his mother for this that he decided to study hard and prove to her that he was really clever. So he never missed his lessons at home, and he became very interested in them, especially in science and history. He read many books about these subjects, and as time went on, his knowledge grew.

Then, when Al was twelve, a railway was opened between Port Huron and Detroit. Al went to see the first train on the new railway puff out of the tiny station. He had never seen a train before, and as he watched it he had a longing to ride in it.

While he stood and pondered as to how he could get a ride, an idea struck him. He ran home to tell it to his mother. Breathlessly he ran up to her and said, "Mother, I have just been to look at the new railway. I have a longing to go on the train, and I thought that maybe I could get a job on it. Can I go to work there if I can get a job?"

"To work?" queried his mother. "You have no need to work. Your father provides enough money to keep you for a few years yet. You are too young to think about working. Run along and play."

"But, mother, I want to work on the train. It will be more fun than work."

"Well, if I let you go, what kind of a job do you think a youngster like you can get? Surely you do not expect to be a driver?" went on his mother.

"Why, no. I've got a marvellous idea. I've planned to buy a stock of sweets and newspapers and sell them to the passengers on the journey. The profits will make my wages. What do you think of that?"

But his mother only laughed at his silly idea and told him to run along and forget it. Al did run along—but only as far as the railway manager's office. He had made up his mind to get this job. He had difficulty in getting to see the manager, but eventually he was shown into the office.

The manager regarded him with a questioning smile and asked:

"Well, my lad, and what is this urgent business you want to see me about?"

"I want a job on your railway, sir," replied Al nervously. "I thought you might let me travel on your trains to sell sweets and newspapers to the passengers. I've worked out the idea and I think I could do a good trade. The profits I make will do as wages."

At this the manager leaned back in his chair and laughed heartily. "You amuse me, young man, with your quaint idea. But I am afraid you are too young for such work. Come and see me again when you are fifteen, and I will think it over then. You certainly seem to be a bright lad."

But Al was not satisfied. He was determined to have his wish. So he pleaded, "But, sir, I want to start working now, or some one else will use my idea before me. Please give me a trial."

The manager rubbed his chin thoughtfully for a few

moments, while Al sat nervously awaiting his answer. Then, with a smile on his face, he said, "All right, you deserve a trial for your persistence. I will see how you get on. Go and buy your sweets and things, and try your luck on to-morrow's train."

"Oh, thank you, sir," cried Al joyfully as he ran out of the office to tell his mother the great news.

So as the gaily painted train drew out of Port Huron next morning, Al was in the luggage-van practising his call of "Sweets, pea-nuts, chewing-gum, and news-papers." When the passengers had settled in their seats, Al walked down the coaches shouting his cry, "Any newspapers or candy. Chewing-gum or pea-nuts."

Four hours later Al stepped off the train at Detroit, tired but happy. On his first journey he had sold all his stock except for a few newspapers. His idea had been successful so far. He then rushed off to another newspaper office to arrange for a daily supply of papers to carry on the train on its return journeys to Port Huron.

So Al continued to make the two train journeys daily, never failing to do a good trade with his wares. About two months later another train was put on the line, and Al, with his eye to business, employed another boy to sell his goods on that. He was continually having new ideas to increase his business. He began to sell fresh fruit and butter, buying them from the farmers and selling to the people at the stations where the train stopped. Very soon; to the admiration of all, this boy was earning far more money each week than most men.

All his profits he used to buy chemicals and books about science and apparatus for his laboratory. He still spent most of his spare time experimenting and increasing his knowledge.

One day Alva had another bright idea. He had noticed that his newspapers sold much more quickly if they contained exciting news, so he went to the printer and offered to pay him for any exciting news, providing he got it well before it was printed in the papers. The first bit of advance news was of a great battle which was then raging in a part of America. As soon as Al got it he rushed off to the station and got the telegraph operator to send it to each station along the line, asking that.it be chalked on boards with the notice that a full account would be found in the papers that were coming on the next train. Knowing that there would be many more people at each station waiting to buy papers, Al went back to the newspaper office to order more than his usual supply.

He said to the clerk, "I shall want a thousand newspapers to-day instead of my usual three hundred."

The clerk asked, "Where is your money to pay for them?"

"I will pay to-morrow."

"Then I cannot let you have them. It is too big an order to let you have without payment."

Alva had no time to argue with this clerk, so he ran upstairs and found the editor, who listened to his story intently as he told him of his latest idea. Realizing that Alva might sell many more copies of his paper regularly, the editor thought it worth the risk to let him have them for once without paying for them, so he said, "You go back to your train, and I promise that you will get your thousand papers."

True to his word, the editor sent boys down to the train, just before it was due to start, with bundles of papers, which were thrown into the luggage-van. As the train pulled out of the station Al stood nervously twitching his fingers, wondering whether his idea would work. Would the papers sell as he had hoped, or would he be left with hundreds which he could not pay for?

His fears were soon relieved, however, for at the first

stop he sold more than fifty papers, whereas he usually sold only two. As each stop was made there were people on the platform clamouring to get a paper. The bundles in the luggage-van became fewer and fewer. At each succeeding stop Alva raised the price, and before the train arrived at Port Huron he had earned a lot of money. It had been a clever idea for one so young.

At about this time, in the year 1862, Alva found a friend named Jimmy Clancy, who was also interested in science. They began to experiment together to build a telegraph set to send messages over wires in morse code. Telegraphy was quite a new invention at that time, and only the railway used it to send messages from one station to another. The two boys made many experiments, using such materials as bottles and rags for insulators, wire from stove-pipes, and copper plates for batteries from wash-boiler bottoms.

Then, when the instruments were finished, the two boys rigged up wires between their homes. Late one evening they arranged to test their apparatus. Alva excitedly seated himself before his home-made batteries and tapping-key at the appointed time and started sending out messages. Full of anxiety lest he should get no reply from Jimmy, he waited breathlessly. Then, to his joy, came a faint tap-tap in his ears, and he knew that it was Jimmy's reply. Their telegraph was working! After this first success, the two boys spent many hours each night sending messages to each other.

After a few nights, however, Alva's father found out— and he was not so pleased with their success! Going down into the laboratory one night, he said to Alva:

"What do you mean by this? It is past twelve o'clock. Get off to bed at once, and see that you are there in future no later than half-past eleven. You would sit up all night to play about if I let you."

"But, father, I don't finish selling my papers until eleven o'clock each night, and there won't be time to make my experiments."

"I can't help that. You need more sleep than you are getting," persisted his father.

But Alva's nimble brain soon thought of a way to make his father change his mind. It was usual for him to bring home each night any unsold papers for his father to read. So on the following night he took them round to Jimmy's instead and told his father he had sold out.

"What a nuisance!" answered Mr Edison. "Now I shall miss all the news. Surely you could have saved me one."

Then Alva, starting up and pretending that a bright idea had just come into his head, exclaimed, "I know! Let us send a message with my telegraph to Jimmy. His father might know the news, and Jimmy can telegraph it back."

His father laughed at this suggestion but agreed to try it out. They went down into the laboratory, and after a few moments, greatly to Mr Edison's surprise, Alva began to receive the news on his simple apparatus. Of course Jimmy and Alva had arranged it all beforehand.

It took a long time to receive the news in morse code, and before Mr Edison realized it the time was past one o'clock. This performance was carried on for three nights before Mr Edison suddenly realized how he had been tricked into letting Alva stay up late to experiment with his telegraph. But he was decent about it and promised to let Alva stay up late in future if he brought him a newspaper each night.

One day Alva was standing on the platform at a station called Mount Clemens selling his newspapers. The station-master's little child was playing on the line, when suddenly a coach broke away from the train and began to run towards the child, gathering speed as it went. Alva, seeing the danger, threw down his papers and, without hesitation, sprang on to the line in the path of the oncoming coach. Quickly he grabbed the child and sprang to one side just as the coach came clattering past. He had risked his own life to save the child by a matter of seconds.

Naturally the station-master was extremely grateful to Alva, and he said:

"I would dearly like to give you a reward for your courage, but my wages are low, and I only have sufficient to feed my family. What else could I give you?"

"I want nothing, sir, for what I did," answered Alva; "but if you would really like to help me, I will ask you to teach me how to use your telegraph instrument."

"That I will gladly do," replied the station-master.

So twice a day, when the train stopped at Mount Clemens, Alva would run into the station-office to have his lesson in telegraphy. Then one day some weeks later, to the station-master's surprise, Alva came to the office with a set of instruments which he had made himself. The station-master tried them and found that they worked quite as well as the expensive ones installed at the station. He congratulated Alva on his cleverness.

All this time Alva's train-business continued to flourish. Walking in Detroit one day, he saw in a shop-window an old hand-printing press for sale. It gave him another idea. Without hesitation he bought it, took it back to his train, and fixed it up in the luggage-van. As soon as he had learnt by experimenting how it worked, he began to put his idea into practice. He began to print a newspaper of his own!

This was the first newspaper that was ever printed on a train. He obtained late news at each station as the train stopped, set it into type, and sold the papers at succeeding stations. These papers soon sold as fast as he could print them. He wrote witty articles to fill up the pages. These articles were so true that they sometimes offended the readers—so much so that one day one of these angry readers tried to catch Alva to give him a spanking. But Alva was too quick for him. He ran away as the reader set off in chase of him. But Alva was out of luck! He had run towards a river, and there was no way of escape except by swimming across. The angry reader was still after him, so he dived into the icy water, fully clothed, and swam to the opposite bank. Cold and shivering, Alva climbed wearily up the bank and sat down to ponder. He decided that newspaper-printing was no job for him; it got him into too many scrapes. He resolved to finish with his train-work and become an expert telegraphist.

His lessons with the station-master served him to good purpose. He easily found a job as an operator. In order to improve his knowledge he changed his job every few months. The work took him to various towns, and wherever he moved he took with him his tools and chemicals, so that he could continue his experiments in his spare time. In one town he obtained a post of night telegraphist in a large office, and he spent most of the daytime working in his rooms, making and experimenting. He did not like night work very much; he found it very difficult to keep awake to do his work. It was part of his duty to ring a bell every hour so that his chief at another office would receive the message and know that he was still attending to his work and had not fallen asleep. Alva—or Tom, as people had now taken to calling him— thought and wondered how he could make the bell ring even if he did fall asleep. After a few days of experiments he took to the office a little gadget which he had invented. It contained a notched wheel which could be attached both to his telegraph instrument and to a clock. Once an hour the wheel revolved, causing the bell to give a signal to his chief. A great idea, thought Tom. But unfortunately his device did not serve him long, for one night, just after it had given its signal, the chief signalled back. Tom, being asleep, did not answer. The chief thought this strange, so he sent a man to investigate. When he found out what had been done, Tom lost his job.

He soon obtained another post as first-class telegraphist with a large company called the Western Union. The manager of the office soon noticed Tom's cleverness at inventing and making electrical gadgets, so he gave him the use of a room in the basement to carry out his experiments. Here he spent many weeks trying to invent a method of sending two messages over one wire at the same time.

His fellow-workers laughed at him when they heard what he was trying to do, and a director named General Coleman said to him, "Any fool knows that a wire can't be worked both ways at once. You are wasting your time on such a mad idea."

Tom, undisturbed by the jeers and laughs, just went on experimenting. Somehow he was sure that his idea would work if only he could make the instruments as he wanted them. Then he was transferred to the Boston office of the same company. Here he spent every spare minute working on his idea of sending two messages at once over a wire.

Eventually he got his device working and showed it to his workmates. They were astonished at its efficiency and predicted that it would become the greatest invention ever known.

The next morning some of the newspapers printed articles about Thomas Edison and his great invention. Buying a dozen copies, he waved them excitedly in front of a friend of his and exclaimed, "I am going to send these to General Coleman to let him know that a fool has at last made a wire work both ways at once."

Soon after this he invented another machine for recording votes at elections. He thought it a good idea and hoped to make a lot of money from it. He showed it to an election committee, feeling sure that they would jump at the chance to buy it, but they disappointed him by saying, "If there is anything on earth we do not want, it is a machine like this. The voters can very well use their hands without our going to the expense of that."

Tom took his machine home and smashed it up, so angry was he at wasting so much time on making something that nobody wanted. Thereupon he vowed, "Never again will I invent a thing unless I am sure it is really wanted."

Tom now gave up his work as telegraphist to devote his whole time to inventing. He first tried to sell his double telegraph transmitter, but forgetting to patent it, found his idea stolen by another inventor. Disappointed and without money, he was at a loss to know what to do. Then, luckily, he met another electrician named Franklin Pope who had some money, and they arranged to start a business as electrical engineers.

They began by installing private telegraph lines into business-houses. Edison was all the while introducing new ideas and inventions into their system of telegraphy. Business flourished. They were taking business away from rival electricians, and eventually a man named Lefferts, who was worried at his declining business, offered Edison and Pope fifteen thousand dollars for their inventions if Edison would work for him. The partners accepted this offer, but Tom was not better off for money, because he sent his share to his father, who had recently fallen on hard times.

So Tom started to work for Lefferts, inventing and improving electrical devices. He was already being talked about as a rising inventor when one day Lefferts said to him, "I want to buy all your inventions which you did not sell with your business. How much do you want for them?"

Tom thought quickly. He had many little inventions which he had never made any use of, but were they worth anything? But he was in need of money. Would three thousand dollars be too much, he wondered. But unable to decide for himself, he replied:

"How much are you prepared to give me, sir?"

"Well, I had thought of forty thousand dollars. Would that be enough?"

Tom staggered. It was a fortune. He could hardly believe his ears, but he managed to stammer:

"I shall be quite satisfied if you are, sir."

Tom was only twenty-three when he received this money, and with it he started a business at Newport, near New York, for making and selling his future inventions.

One day Professor Morse, the inventor of the code and the first telegraph, asked Tom to go with him to see a new engine worked by electricity which had recently been invented by another engineer.

Watching this wonderful machine drive a circular saw, Professor Morse delightedly exclaimed, "What a marvellous invention! I am thankful to have lived to see it. Now we shall be able to use electricity to drive machinery."

Edison did not answer. He stood listening intently to the hum of the machine. He did not seem satisfied. Then suddenly, diving down to look under the motor, he exclaimed, "This invention is a fraud! It is being worked by a belt from a steam-engine in a room below."

226

His quick ears and alert eyes had noticed sounds in the running of the motor which sounded like those of a steam-engine. Morse could hardly believe his eyes when he saw the belt below, and he said to Edison, "I should

"FORTY THOUSAND DOLLARS"

never have detected the fraud, young man. I am sorry to have brought you here."

But Tom replied, "I am not sorry to have come. It has, at least, set my mind working on a fresh idea. Some day I will invent a motor that will really work by electricity."

The news of the discovery of this fraud helped to make

the name of Edison famous. Every paper was talking about his remarkable skill as an inventor. The amount of work he was doing was enormous. It is said that, at the age of twenty-four, he was working at no fewer than forty-five different inventions.

So greatly had he improved the telegraph that, by the year 1875, people were talking of the possibilities of a telegraph that could speak. Edison had begun experiments on it, and two other inventors, Graham Bell and Elisha Gray, were also putting all their energies into similar experiments. They could all see that a fortune awaited the man who was first to make a workable one.

Edison worked day and night on his idea, making delicate instruments, altering and adjusting them. But just as he seemed to have neared success, Bell patented a similar idea. Edison was so disgusted at being too slow that he discontinued his experiments and turned to other things. Gray was even more unfortunate than Edison, for he was ready to patent his telephone only a few hours after Bell had patented his.

Actually, if Edison had kept on working at his telephone he might have been the inventor of wireless long before it was thought of by other people. His experiments had been leading him in that direction. In fact, he sold his patents on his wireless inventions to Marconi twenty years before the latter gave it to the world.

Bell's telephone was a simple affair. The mouthpiece was first spoken into and then used as an earpiece to receive the answer. Edison tested it and quickly realized that there was much room for improvement in it. So he set about working upon it. He first decided that separate mouth- and ear-pieces were necessary, and that the sounds must be much more distinct if people were to use the telephone regularly. He experimented with many materials for transmitting clear sounds, such as drops of water, felt, sponges, moistened paper, and graphite.

But Bell was also working on improvements. He had already managed to telephone to his assistant over a distance of more than two miles. Edison had many

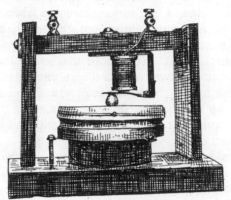

BELL'S TELEPHONE

failures, but he was undaunted. He was convinced that he could work out his ideas eventually.

He wrote to his father at this time, "I have had hard luck with my speaking telegraph, but I think it is all right now. I am hard up for money at the moment, having spent all my time at this invention and neglecting my other work. But if I am successful I shall soon be earning a lot of money."

The big telegraph firms were closely watching the progress of the various experimenters. They were each waiting to buy up the best 'speaking telegraph' for themselves. Hearing of Edison's remarkable progress, the manager of Western Union offered him a hundred and fifty dollars a week for first claim on his inventions when they were complete. Edison accepted, and a month later he patented his new telephone. After this there continued much friendly rivalry between Edison, Bell, and Gray. Each kept inventing more improvements, and the telephone gradually developed into the wonderful instrument as we know it to-day.

One day in 1877 Edison was experimenting with an electrical machine he had just constructed when he placed two wires to the wrong connexions. Suddenly a grooved disc on the machine began whizzing round, scratching against a metal point. He noticed that as the metal point slipped into the grooves on the disc, a variety of different sounds were heard. These strange sounds puzzled him. He stayed up all night to find the reason for this occurrence. He could not rest until he had satisfied himself as to the cause:

Then, suddenly, he thought to himself, "I wonder if I could make a machine which would talk? I will find out by experimenting."

It sounded preposterous at the time, but he settled down to think out an idea. The next day he sent for his chief mechanic, gave him a number of sketches which he had made during the night, and said:

"I want you to build this machine as quickly and as accurately as you can."

The mechanic looked at the sketches with a puzzled frown—he had never seen any like these before—but went off to obey his master. A week passed by, and then one morning the mechanic came back with the weird-looking machine in his arms. He placed it before Edison and queried, "Now we have made it, what is it supposed to do?"

Edison briefly answered, "It has got to talk."

The mechanic looked at Edison strangely. Had the man gone mad? A machine which would talk! It was so ridiculous.

When the other workmen heard what Edison had said they chaffed and joked about it. They thought Edison must have been playing a joke on them. So they all gathered round Edison as he prepared to test his new

THE FIRST PHONOGRAPH

machine. They waited to see it fail to work, so that they could have a good laugh at their master's expense.

Edison, knowing the state of their minds, smiled to himself as he wound up a crank on the machine and slowly recited, in a loud voice, the nursery rhyme, "Mary had a little lamb." Then, turning back the crank to its original place, he repeated the motion of moving it forward again.

To the astonishment of everybody, except the inventor

himself, the machine began to echo the rhyme in exactly the same tone that Edison had previously recited it. Excitement grew high. The workmen were no longer in a laughing mood. They were too amazed and staggered at this marvellous new creation of their master's. Now it was his turn to laugh. The machine did talk!

For weeks afterwards the newspapers were filled with details of this new invention and of its brilliant inventor. It was given the name of phonograph, which was, as you know, later changed to gramophone.

Everybody wanted to hear it working. Edison demonstrated it before a meeting of the great American scientists who were loud in their praise of it. Then he had the great honour of taking it to Washington to show it to the President of the United States. Again he received a great ovation. Crowds were now continually swarming round his laboratory to get a glimpse of this great inventor. But for all the fame and success that came his way, Edison still thought only of inventing and constructing electrical apparatus. His experiments were now leading him in another direction—that of using electricity to give light. Only a few scientists, at that time, could see the possibility of lighting by electricity, and most people jeered at the idea as being ridiculous.

Eighteen years earlier an inventor named Swan had constructed a crude lamp with carbon rods in a glass bottle. It did give some light, but it used too much electricity to be put to practical use. Edison saw this lamp and decided to try to improve upon it. He was one of the few people who could see its possibilities. But shortly after starting experiments, the Western Union began worrying him to finish a new telephone system which he had promised them. So he had to put the lighting-experiments on one side for a time. He worked at the telephone until satisfied with its performance, and then sold it to the Western Union for the immense sum of one hundred thousand dollars.

When the newspapers heard that Edison had resumed his experiments with lighting, they printed the news that electricity would shortly replace gas for lighting-purposes. The gas-companies were soon up in arms against Edison. They were afraid their businesses would have to close. So they set about ridiculing the idea, saying that it was impossible to light with electricity and that Edison was nothing more than an idle boaster. Edison took little notice of these jibes and set about finding money to start a new business for experimenting with his lighting. He persuaded a number of wealthy men to lend him money, and the Edison Electric Light Company was formed.

Weeks went by, but nobody heard any news of an advance in his experiments. People began to think Edison was bluffing and could not accomplish what he had set out to do. His wealthy friends began to think that they were going to lose the money they had lent to start the business, and one of them asked Edison:

"Are you sure that you can make light with electricity? Or are you wasting your time and our money? We are getting tired of waiting for something to happen."

"Of course I am sure," replied Edison crossly. "When I am ready I will show you a light which will need no match to light it, which will not blaze nor flicker, which will be whiter than any gas-light, and which will be clean and dustless. But I must be given time to improve it before it is shown to the world."

The man went away satisfied, but the papers continued to print protest after protest about Edison's slackness.

Then, in April, 1879, he was ready to take out a patent for his light-bulb. But he meant to startle the world with his new discovery. He would show the people who had sneered at him what a big mistake they had made. So he got a newspaper to prepare a long illustrated article about his lamps, offering to give a demonstration of them at his works on a certain date. The article aroused such a stir of excitement that on the appointed day thousands upon thousands flocked to Edison's laboratory to see the demonstration. There were continual expressions of delight and astonishment from those who were able to squeeze into the rooms to see the wonderful lights suspended from the ceilings.

The name of Edison was on everybody's tongue. Telegrams and letters of praise poured in upon him. He had convinced the world of his great genius.

But the English scientist Swan had not been idle. He had been working on the lamp he had invented twenty years before. He was now perfecting a lamp similar to Edison's. English papers were saying that it was far better than Edison's. Other inventors had also been busy stealing ideas and were claiming the honour of inventing the lamp.

Then came a big exhibition in Paris, where all the inventors were asked to demonstrate their lamps. Edison triumphed. His lamps were judged by far the best there, and he was awarded the Diploma of Honour.

After this, for the remainder of his life, Edison went from triumph to triumph in the world of craftsmanship and invention. His great achievements with the telegraph, telephone, gramophone, and electric light were only a few of the benefits his clever hands and brain gave to the world. Some of his other notable inventions were the motion-picture camera, the electric railway, the microphone, and the electric motor.

So great was his fame that in 1922 the people of America voted him to be the greatest living American.

He died in 1931 at the ripe old age of eighty-four,

having lived one of the busiest and most fruitful lives ever known.

So when you are using your telephone or wireless set, or finding pleasure at the cinema or with your gramophone or warming yourself before an electric fire, be thankful to this great craftsman and inventor, who lived to make all these things possible.